German Immigration to America

The First Wave

Edited by
Don Heinrich Tolzmann

HERITAGE BOOKS
2007

HERITAGE BOOKS

AN IMPRINT OF HERITAGE BOOKS, INC.

Books, CDs, and more—Worldwide

For our listing of thousands of titles see our website
at
www.HeritageBooks.com

Published 2007 by
HERITAGE BOOKS, INC.
Publishing Division
65 East Main Street
Westminster, Maryland 21157-5026

International Standard Book Number: 978-1-55613-797-6

Contents

Preface   v

Introduction   vii

1. The German Exodus to England in 1709
   by Frank Reid Diffenderffer

2. The German Emigration to America, 1709-1740
   by Henry Eyster Jacobs

Preface

In 1708, representatives of the first major wave of German immigrants arrived upon American shores. By that time, Germans had already been coming to America for a century, but this was the date associated with the first major wave - the first of many that would follow.

The purpose of this work is to shed light on the history of this important event in the history of immigration and settlement in America. It addresses the question as to why the German immigration suddenly became a massive population movement. To accomplish this goal, the editor has selected two essential works, which illuminate this topic.

DHT

Introduction

In 1608, the first German settlers arrived at
Jamestown, Virginia, thus marking the beginning
date in German-American history, and in 1683 group
immigration began with the arrival of the first group
of German immigrants, who established the first
permanent German settlement in America at
Germantown, Pennsylvania. (1) The stage was
thereby set for the beginnings of the German
immigration on a massive scale, and this occurred in
the early 1700s with the immigration from southwest
Germany, especially from the Palatinate.

The significance of this immigration cannot
be underestimated as it in essence became the core
group of the entire colonial German element. (2)

Although the core group of immigrants
actually came from the Palatinate, most German
immigrants were indiscriminately referred to as
"Palatines," since most of them came, if not from the
Palatinate, then from neighboring regions of the
southwestern German-speaking area of Europe,
which included southwest Germany, Alsace-
Lorraine, and Switzerland.

The southwest region of the German-
speaking realm was frequently a battleground during
European warfare. It was repeatedly attacked,
pillaged, and devastated in a period ranging from the
Thirty Years War for the next two centuries through
the Napoleonic era. (3)

The ravages of the Thirty Years War (1618-48) were particularly acute in this region. And after the war, the French burned the castle of Heidelberg and the city of Mannheim. The population was reduced to poverty - America appeared on the horizon as a ray of hope and the chance for a new life. (4)

There are a number of causes and reasons which can be cited as leading to the first wave of immigration, but the single most frequently mentioned one was the devastation caused by the long history of warfare. Indeed, the southwest German-speaking realm may be referred to as a war zone. After the Thirty Years War the region was often the stamping ground for the armies of Louis XIV of France.

It should be noted that the German states were not unified in a centralized state, but its neighbor, France, was, and after 1648 it conducted a foreign policy aimed at direct intervention in German affairs with two quite specific objectives in mind. First, it aimed at obtaining a frontier on the Rhine, which translated into French control of the German-speaking province of Alsace-Lorraine. Second, France aimed at the maintenance of a weak and divided Germany. As a result of the French drive to the east, Germany suffered continual territorial losses: Alsace was annexed by France in 1681; Burgundy was ceded to France in 1714, and Lorraine annexed in 1766.

Margrave Ludwig Wilhelm of Baden remarked with reference to the French conquest of of Alsace in 1681: "For France it is a door constantly open for war, through which she can invade German soil as often as she wishes." And invade France did repeatedly, resulting in the ruination of the southwestern German region, especially the Palatinate. Specifically, the French devastated the province in 1674; in 1688-89 it was laid waste again; and in 1707, during the War of Spanish Succession, it was again plundered. All of this ruination, it should be noted, followed hard on the heels of the Thirty Years War, from which the region had not as yet recovered in 1674, when it was plundered again. By the early 1700s, there had been almost a century of intermittent warfare.

When immigrants were asked about their reasons for immigrating they spoke mainly "of the French ravages in 1707." Hence, the question as to the relationship between French military invervention and aggression in the German states and the beginnings of massive German immigration can best be answered by describing the two as cause and effect. Without the former, it is highly unlikely that the early 1700s would have witnessed the beginnings of the first massive wave of German immigration. (5)

In 1708, the Rev. Joshua Kocherthal applied to an English agency in Frankfurt am Main for permission to take a small group to England, where he applied to Queen Anne for assistance for the Palatines. He recited the cause of their plight as the

French ravages and destruction in southwest Germany. "In the judgement of the immigrants, so severe was the destruction that they could not possibly attain sufficient means of livelihood during the hard times, which still continued." (6) Queen Anne there provided for their welfare and sustenance. Kocherthal then asked if he could transport the Palatine Germans to America. It was decided that New York would be the appropriate place for them.

In 1708, a small group arrived in New York. Each person received fifty acres of land. Among this group were carpenters, smiths, weavers, and various skilled craftsmen. They established a settlement, Newburgh, in New York.

In 1709, there were some 13,000 Germans in England who were awaiting passage to America. In 1710, Kochertal returned to England and brought more of them to America; some of these early Palatine Germans, it should be noted, settled in Ireland, but the majority made it to the New World.

Perhaps the largest group, approximately 3,000, came to New York in 1710. Eventually, it is estimated that tens of thousands came in the colonial period to America, and settled in various colonies.

Among these early German-Amerians were some outstanding individuals, such as John Peter Zenger, the first champion of the free press in America. In New Jersey, two prominent representatives of this group were General Frederick

Frelinghysen and Johann Peter Rockefeller. The former would serve in the American Revolution and become a member of the Continental Congress, the Constitutional Convention, and the U.S. Senate in the 1790s. Rockefeller, of course, became the founder of one of America's most illustrious industrial dynasties. (7)

In America, the Palatines established a variety of towns and villages with German names, such as Weiserdorf, Hartmannsdorf, Brunnendorf, Schmidtdorf, Gerlachsdorf etc. In times of peace, they were regarded as excellent farmers who provided grain and crops for the growing colonies. During the frontier wars and the American Revolution, they acted as a protective bulwark on the frontier, and also actively supported the War of American Independence. (8)

As the representatives of the first massive wave of German immigration to America, the Palatines occupy an important place in American, as well as German-American history. Once underway, the waves of immigration would bring a total of eight millions from the German-speaking countries to America. (9)

This work presents the story of how the century old German immigration in 1709 suddenly experienced the first major wave in a movement that would eventually bring millions to the New World.

Notes

1. See Don Heinrich Tolzmann, *The First Germans in America, With A Biographical Directory of New York Germans* (Bowie, Maryland: Heritage Books, Inc., 1992).

2. A contemporary journal, published in Columbus, Ohio by the Palatines to America Society, which deals with the history and heritage of the Palatines, is *The Palatine Immigrant*, edited by Dr. John Terence Golden.

3. Regarding the Palatine immigration, see Walter Allen Knittle, *Early Eighteenth Century Palatine Emigration* (Baltimore: Genealogicl Pub. Co., 1976).

4. See Don Heinrich Tolzmann, *Germany and America, 1450-1700: Julius Friedrich Sachse's History of the German Role in the Discovery, Exploration, and Settlement of the New World* (Bowie, Maryland: Heritage Books, Inc., 1991). See especially pp. 143-68 for a discussion of "The French Wars of Conquest."

5. For further information on the background of the German immigration, see the editor's "Understanding the Causes of the German Immigrations: The Context of German History Before 1830," in: Don Heinrich Tolzmann, *Das Ohiotal - The Ohio Valley: The German Dimension* (New York: Lang, 1992), pp. 3-17.

6. Knittle, p. 34. A history of the Palatines in New
York notes with regard to the Palatinate, that after the
Thirty Years War, war again broke out in 1668, and
in 1673 Louis XIV of France began his marauding
expeditions...Destructive raids laid waste the Palatine
countryside, ad thi ruthless pillage continued...when
the French King himself entered the land 'to make it
a wilderness,' as he declared. As a youth of twenty
years Kocherthal heard of the burning of Heidelberg
and Mannheim and in May of 1689 news reached
him that Speyer and Worms had been set on fire. The
villages, towns and farms of the Rhine regions were
pillaged and burned, their inhabitants tortured,
ravished or slain." By 1705, England, Holland,
Sweden, and Prussia threatened intervention unless
the carnage stopped which was then taking place
during the War of Spanish Succession (1701-13).
See Lou D. MacWethy, *The Book of Names,
Especially Relating to the Early Palatines and the
First Settlers in the Mohawk Valley* (Baltimore:
Genealogical Pub. Co., 1969), p. 53.

7. See Don Heinrich Tolzmann, *America's German
Hertage* (Cleveland: German-American National
Congress, 1976), pp. 26-27.

8. For further information with regard to the
American Revolution, see Don Heinrich Tolzmann,
*German-Americans in the American Revolution:
Henry Melchior Muhlenberg Richards' History*
(Bowie, Maryland: Heritage Books, Inc., 1992).

9. For a general survey of German-American history, see LaVern J. Rippley, *The German-Americans* (Boston: Twayne, 1976).

1. The German Exodus to England in 1709

By

Frank Reid Diffenderffer

This chapter is a facsimile of material which appeared as: Frank Reid Diffenderffer, "The German Exodus to England in 1709," *Pennsylvania German Society Proceedings and Addresses* 7(1897).

Contents

Introductory 257

1. Immigration Begins 260

2. The German Exodus to England in 1709 264

3. Causes Leading to the Exodus 276

4. The Stay in England 293

5. The German Colony in Ireland 328

6. Conclusion 340

7. Cost of Maintaining These Germans 343

Appendix 347

INTRODUCTORY.

INSIGNIA OF THE PENNSYL-
VANIA-GERMAN SOCIETY.

THE colonization of this continent by the Spaniards, English, Dutch, Swedes, French and Germans, presents many curious historical features and incidents. From the settlement of the Spaniards in Central and South America, to that of the French in the Canadas, many curious episodes thrust themselves upon the consideration of the chronicler, matching in interest and importance anything told in Greek or Roman story. Our Society, while taking an interest in all these early colonists, has to do only with those peoples from whom our membership claims descent, except in so far as they may incidentally have come into contact with the people of other races and their own lives and careers been influenced by the men of other lands, and whose interests and destinies were more or less closely interwoven with their own.

But even as we stand upon the very threshold of this great question of Germanic immigration and settlement in the New World, we are confronted with the magnitude no less than the importance and grandeur of the subject. Its period of active and continuous duration covers more than a century, and even now, more than two centuries since the first German settlement was made in one of the suburbs of Philadelphia, this Teutonic wave still continues to reach the shores of our Commonwealth. De Quincy in one of his brilliant essays describes the flight of a Tartar tribe, in which 600,000 men, women and children, pursued their course from the banks of the Volga, for more than 2000 miles through the treeless plains and sandy wastes that mark the highlands of Central Asia, from midwinter until the succeeding fall. It was an event wonderful in its conception and as remarkable for its successful execution. But it was after all, only the return of a people to the home which their forefathers had left generations before. It was going back to the old rooftrees where plenty as well as a welcome awaited them. Not so with the early Germans who came to America. Desolation and hunger indeed, lay behind them. With poverty and misery for companions, they braved the perils of the ocean for months at a time ; they were crowded into ships that became pest houses, in which the fatal

ship fever more than decimated their ranks, the survivors well aware that years of servitude under task
masters would be their lot.

But the task to which I address myself is not to
rehearse the story of the German immigration and
settlement in this and some of the other states.
That is a grand theme, worthy of anyone's ambition.
In a general way it has been told and retold, but the
subject is of fadeless interest and much still remains
to be discovered and recorded. Out of the many interesting phases of this wonderful story, I have
chosen one episode, one of which the writers of our
history have made but small account, but which,
while surrounded by obscurity, is nevertheless of sur-
passing interest to us, the descendants of those early
colonists.

IMMIGRATION BEGINS.

EARLY GERMAN COLONISTS TO AMERICA—WHEN AND WHERE
LOCATED—FOLLOWED BY THE STILL GREATER IMMIGRA-
TION IN THE SUMMER OF 1709 TO LONDON, MUCH OF
WHICH EVENTUALLY FOUND ITS WAY INTO PENNSYLVANIA.

 *T* HERE has been some discus-
sion among historians who
have dealt with the question of
German immigration to America,
which should be considered the
first established colony. Löher[1]
tells us the Spaniards, Italians,
French and English may not claim the exclusive
honor of founding early settlements on this continent. "In Veuezuela was planted the first German colony in the New World," are his words.[2]

---

[1] Geschichte und Zustanden der Deutchen in Amerika, von Franz
Löher, p. 1. This now well-established fact has also been carefully
elaborated by Julius F. Sachse, Esq.

[2] Geschichte, p. 14.

The date given is 1526. The colony which settled itself on the shores of the Delaware in 1638, while ostensibly Swedish, was largely composed of Germans. Although Gustavus Adolphus and his no less illustrious minister, Axel Oxenstierna, were its promoters, the great Protestant king begged the Protestant German princes to permit their subjects to join his scheme of colonization,[3] and from the names among those colonists that have come down to us, we are assured that many of them were Germans. The charter accorded the Germans even more favorable conditions than it did to the Swedes themselves. Campanius, the earliest Swedish historian of New Sweden, tells us Germans went in the ship "der Vogel Greif" which sailed with 50 colonists to establish the first colony on the Delaware. In 1638, Peter Minnewit, the first Governor, was drowned in the West Indies. Johannes Printz, a native of Holstein, succeeded him. Although Printz was in the Swedish service, he was a German nobleman whose full name was Edler von Buchan. With Printz came 54 German families, mostly from Pomerania.[4] These facts establish the semi-German character of this so-called Swedish colony.

But when we come to look for a German colony in the New World that was distinctively such, that was permanent in its nature and left its imprint in

---

[3] Mr. Provost Stille, in Penna. Mag. of Hist. and Biog.

[4] The First German Immigrants to North America, by Louis P. Hennighausen, pp. 160-162.

ineffaceable characters upon the future of the people of Pennsylvania, we must re-echo the words of the late Dr. Seidensticker who said: "Should it be asked when the German immigration in America had its beginning, the answer must be, in the year 1683."[5] He of course alludes to the Germantown settlement.

From that time forward, individuals and families found their way to the New World, but this immigration for some years was small and sporadic. We do not find that colonies of any considerable size made their way hither. In 1705 a number of German Reformed families left their homes between Wolfenbuttel and Halberstadt. They first went to Neuwied, in Rheinish Prussia, and thence to Holland, whence they sailed for New York, and finally settled in German Valley, Morris county, New Jersey.[6]

A still more important German colony was led to these shores in 1708. In January of that year, Joshua von Kocherthal, a German preacher, representing 21 families, composed of 54 persons,[7] presented himself to the resident English government agent, Davenant, at Frankfort-on-the-Main, and asked for permission to go to England, as well as for the necessary subsistence. Davenant consulted with

---

[5] "Fragt mann welcher zeit die deutsche Einwannderung in America ihren Anfang genommen habe, so lautet die Antwort: Im Jahre 1683." Bilder aus der Deutche-Pennsylvanischen Geschichte, von Oswald Seidensticker, p. 3.

[6] The Pennsylvania German Dialect, by Dr. Marion Dexter Learned.

[7] Their number is variously stated. Kapp says 61. See his Deutchen im Staate New York, p. 12.

Letter of citizenship granted by the Queen to the members of the Kochert

Colony, the first German one sent out under Government auspices. (See

the home government, and was advised, that no
assistance could be rendered until these people
received the consent of the Elector to expatriate
themselves. Without more ado, Kocherthal and
his little colony of Palatines, in March, made
their way through the Low Countries and across
the sea to London. Upon their arrival they were
completely impoverished and without means of
subsistence. Queen Anne allowed each a stipend
of one shilling per day. What to do with them was
the question. It was at first decided to send them to
the island of Jamaica or Antigua, in the West Indies,
but to this the Palatines objected because the climate
there was so unlike their own. With their consent
their destination was changed to New York, whose
climate was more like that to which they were accustomed. Accordingly, on April 28, 1708, they were
sent to that colony on a government vessel, accompanied by Lord Lovelace, the newly appointed Governor.[8]

---

[8] Die Deutchen im Staate New York, während des achtzehnten Jahr-
hunderts, von Freiderich Kapp. The records of the Board of Trade
show that of this colony 10 were men, 10 women, 21 children, the rest
unclassified. There was 1 joiner, 1 smith, and the rest were farmers, while
the women understood the sams business. An effort was made to salary
Kocherthal, but Secretary Boyle said he could find no authority to
settle a salary on a foreign clergyman, Tools were however furnished
for the colonists, and 20 pounds were given to Kocherthal for books and
clothes. *See records of the Board of Trade.* Appendix B.

ARMS OF THE CITY OF LONDON.

THE GERMAN EXODUS TO ENGLAND IN 1709.

REMARKABLE MOVEMENT OF PALATINES AND SWABIANS TO
LONDON, IN SEARCH OF HOMES IN THE NEW WORLD—THE
MASSEN-AUSWANDERUNG OF THE GERMAN WRITERS—AT-
TEMPT TO TRACE ITS ORIGIN—NO SINGLE CAUSE RESPONSI-
BLE FOR IT.

ARMS OF THE GERMAN EMPIRE, A. D.
1694.

*T*HESE preliminary re-
marks bring me to the
subject which it is the aim
of this paper to bring into
prominence, the remarkable
emigration of Germans,—
Palatines, Swabians and
others,—to London in the
spring and summer of
1709.

As has been seen, there
was up to the beginning of
the eighteenth century, no extended emigration

movement in the direction of the English colonies in America by Germans. It is true, immigrants continued to come in the wake of the Germantown settlers, but they were either a few families at a time, or isolated individuals, and did not attract much attention. This period of comparative quietude continued uninterruptedly until 1709. During the entire period which elapsed from the establishment of the Pastorius colony in 1683 to the year 1709, the immigration was sporadic and unimportant. I have been unable to ascertain with exactness the number of Germans in Pennsylvania in the last named year, but it is almost certain that it did not exceed two or three thousand individuals, which would give us an average immigration of about 100 individuals annually during the entire period, surely a very moderate number when we consider the efforts made by Penn to secure colonists, the favorable reports sent to the old home by the Crefelders, and the wide dispersion of pamphlets throughout Germany, reciting in

---

Through the courtesy of Dr. F. D. Stone, the accomplished librarian of the Pennsylvania Historical Society, I am enabled to present to the American public this fac-simile of the letter of denization granted to the colony of Germans led to this country by the Rev. Joshua von Kocherthal, in 1708. This colony numbered fifty-four persons and was the first one composed of Germans who came across the Atlantic under the direct auspices and with the assistance of the English Government. The sum expended by the Government in planting this little colony in New York, was from first to last £655, of which amount Lord Lovelace's bill was for £202,17,8½. On August 29, 1709, Kocherthal sent a letter of thanks to the Board of Trade for its favor and kind offices. The above fac-simile, I believe, has never been printed or reproduced before.

glowing terms the advantages of Pennsylvania as a land of plenty and an asylum from oppression.

THE FIRST ARRIVALS IN LONDON.

During the months of May and June, 1709, the citizens of the city of London were astonished to find the streets of that metropolis swarming with men and women of an alien race, speaking an unknown tongue and bearing unmistakable indications of poverty, misery and want. It soon became known that about 5000 of these people were sheltered under tents in the suburbs of the city.

Additions were almost daily made to their number during June, July, August and September, and by October, between 13,000 and 14,000 had come. Then this "massen-auswanderung der Pfälzer," as Kapp calls it, gradually drew to a close.

This sudden irruption of so many thousands of foreigners within a few months, into a country where but few of them had ever appeared before, and where they were utter strangers, rather than into neighboring countries of like faith and kindred language, that would perhaps have been more ready to welcome them, stands forth as one of the most remarkable facts of the time. It was found that these people were Germans from the country lying between Landau, Spire and Mannheim, reaching almost to Cologne, commonly called the Palatinate. There were, however, many from other parts of Germany, principally from Swabia and Wurtemberg.

About the manner of their coming we learn more

*Johannes Wilhelmus —
Elector Palatinus.*

from a report made to the House of Commons in 1711, than from any other source. By that report we are told that in the spring of 1709 great numbers of these people came down the Rhine and did not pause until they reached Rotterdam, in Holland. They were even then miserably poor, and were maintained while in that city by the charity of the people. Their destination, however, was England, but for lack of the necessary shipping and want of other means, they were detained in Rotterdam. The English ministry consented to provide the necessary transportation and receive 5000 of their number.[10] Transports and other vessels were accordingly pro-

---

[10] Cassell's History of England. Text by William Howitt.

I am indebted to the courtesy of Julius F. Sachse, Esq., for the portrait of the Elector Palatine, John William, of the House of Newburg, which is here presented. I further avail myself of this opportunity to acknowledge my indebtedness to the same gentleman for other assistance both in the text and illustrations that accompany this article. His wide acquaintance with the pictorial as well as the written history of this period, freely placed at my service, has been of much value to me, and I would be doing an injustice to myself as well as to him, did I not make the fullest acknowledgement of his valuable advice and assistance.

I regret that I have been unable to supply a biography of this ruler. All I have been able to learn about him has been supplied by Protestant sources, and this, of course, has not been of a favorable character. In two lengthy letters written at that time by "A Nobleman," which I found among the papers of the late I. D. Rupp, and addressed to the English people, a long list of accusations are brought against him. The charges are mainly that he had failed to comply with the solemn treaty stipulations he had entered into with his Protestant subjects. There are no accusations of persecutions, but there were other means of manifesting his preference for his Catholic subjects. Probably he was neither better nor worse than the average petty ruler of his day.

vided by the English Government at the charge of the crown.

In one of his official communications to Mr. Secretary Boyle, Mr. Dayrolles, the English Minister at the Hague, informed that person that these immigrants were persuaded to go to England by some one in the latter country, and that even after the coming of any more had been prohibited, "a gentleman with a servant who had come over in a packet boat, had on August 20, 1709, gone to Brühl, a town near Cologne, where large numbers of Palatines were staying, and distributed money among them. Printed tickets were also sent to their friends in Germany to persuade them to do the same." Minister Dayrolles said he could never learn who this mysterious person was, much as he tried to do so. The Committee investigating the matter in England could do no more, but they did find from two letters, that one Henry Torne, a Quaker at Rotterdam, who had been acting under Minister Dayrolles, had forced a great number to embark for England after they had been provided for to return to their own country.[11]

I am strongly inclined to believe from the foregoing, that the Land Companies did not confine their efforts to secure immigration to the dissemination of booklets and other literature having that end in

---

[11] It has been suggested to me that this "unknown" may have been Benjamin Furly, an English Quaker, the life long friend of William Penn, and the promotor of the first German emigration to Pennsylvania. He was born in 1636 and died in 1714.

view, but that they were also operating through agents to persuade these people to cross the ocean and settle upon the rich and virgin lands beyond the ocean. Lord Sunderland, on May 3, 1709, said the Queen was convinced this immigration would greatly benefit her kingdom if some means could be found to settle them comfortable in England, instead of sending them to the West Indies. If, after all, the English ministry was covertly at work and instigating this exodus, they operated so secretly that their fine hand was never discovered.

In June the number sent over had reached more than ten thousand, and the Queen's Government began to be alarmed as there was no cessation, apparently, in the number clamoring to come. Secretary Boyle accordingly sent orders to her Majesty's Minister at the Hague, to prevent any further shipments until those who were already in England, should have been disposed of. To further make this fact known throughout Holland and the Palatinate, advertisements were published in the Dutch Gazettes, that no more would be carried to England. Either the pressure brought to bear on Minister Dayrolles was too strong, or his kind heart was unable to bear up under the impassionate beseechings of these friendless wanderers, so that disregarding his instructions, he sent over nearly three thousand more at Queen Anne's expense, while still others were forwarded by the charitable citizens of Rotterdam, and supplied by them with food, inasmuch as the magistrates of that place no longer permitted the immigrants even to enter the city, which of course served only to intensify their want, their sufferings and their general misery.

But neither the declarations of the English government, nor the indignation of the then Elector Palatine, John William, of the house of Newburg, who was loath to see his subjects leave him, seems to have deterred still others from making an effort to get across the North Sea. Oft repeated orders continued to be sent to the English Minister to prevent or check this exodus. Even Holland itself was appealed to, to issue similar notices, but it would seem nothing was able to stay this wholesale emigration until it had run its course, and the large number I have already mentioned had landed on the English shores. But even then it did not entirely cease. This is shown by a Proclamation or circular issued by the English government as late as the last day of December, 1709, in which further emigration is alluded to, and all persons are absolutely prohibited from coming over from Holland under pain of being immediately sent back to Germany. A fac-simile of this curious Proclamation is herewith given.[11a]

The archives of the city of Rotterdam afford us an excellent insight into the continental side of this emigration. From the records of a meeting of the Burgomasters of that city, held on April 22d, 1709, we learn it was resolved to pay to Engel Kon and Samuel de Back, four hundred and fifty guilders to be distributed among destitute families of the Lower Palatinate, for their subsistence on their journey to

Königl. Englisch in Teutsch=land verschickte Declaration, oder Abmahnungs=Schreiben.

Dnnach letzt verwichenen Sommer/ eine grosse An=zahl armer Leuthe/ von verschiedenen Orten/ aus Teutschland allhier in Engelland angekommen/ welche bißhero von Jhrer Königlichen Majestät unterhalten / und nach und nach/ in West Jndien und nacher Jrr=land versandt worden: Weilen aber der=gleichen armer Leuthe seither mehr an=hero gekommen / und man darauf hin nacher Holland/ und anderwerts Nach=richt gegeben / daß dergleichen keine mehr passirt/ vielweniger unterhalten; die jenige auch/ welche seither dem ersten October letzhin allhier angelanget / wieder mit erster Gelegenheit / zurück über Holland nacher Teutschland gesandt werden sollen. Als wird hierdurch allen denjenigen/ welche noch *intentionirt* sind/ anhero zu kommen / zur Nachricht wis=send gemacht /. solche ihre Reyse ein zu=stellen/. welche gewißlich fruchtloß fal=len wird/ es seydann / daß sie von selb=sten bemittelt sind sich zu unterhal=ten. Datum London den 31. De=cember 1709.

England, and a warrant was ordered for that amount. Seven days afterwards, at another meeting of the town council it was ordered that a warrant should be drawn to pay Peter Toomen three hundred guilders to be distributed among those destitute Germans who came subsequently to those to whom money had already been paid.[12]

But the city of Rotterdam grew tired of spending so much money on these flying columns of Palatines, from whom it could expect no benefit. Accordingly on the 12th of August, 1709, the Burgomasters of the city had eight circulars prepared and distributed, in which public notice was given that the Queen of Great Britain having ordered that no more of these people should be sent over to England, until those already there had in some way been disposed of, two commissioners, Hendrick Toom and Jon van Gent, who, having out of charity taken order by direction of

---

[11a] The following is a translation of the Royal English Declaration or Proclamation (p. 271) transmitted to Germany : ''Inasmuch as during the summer just past a large number of poor people arrived here in England, from different parts of Germany, who have hitherto been supported by Her Royal Majesty, and have gradually been sent to the West Indies, and afterwards to Ireland : and where as more such poor people have come hither since, notice has consequently been sent to Holland and elsewhere that none such would be passed much less supported, and that those also, who have arrived here since the first of last October were to be sent back to Germany via Holland at the first opportunity. All such as intend to come hither are therefore notified to desist from their voyage which would assuredly result in failure unless it be that they have means of their own with which to support themselves. Dated, London, the 31st of December, 1709.''

[12] See Appendix "A" for full detail, quoted from the minutes of the proceedings of the City Council of Rotterdam.

her Majesty to provide transportation and other necessities for these people, should also be instructed to notify all persons who might yet intend to come from Germany, to remain away and prevent them making a fruitless journey.

The two agents just named were instructed to put two yachts on the rivers Waal and Maas and cruise on those streams in order to turn back any emigrants who might be coming down on their way to Rotterdam and England. It was stated that they had already stopped one thousand and turned them back. The council on August 24, allowed them three hundred and fifty guilders for their services. The Burgomasters of the city of Brielle, a fortified town in South Holland, also adopted a scheme to shift the burden of supporting some of these people from their own shoulders. They wrote a letter to the Rotterdam authorities stating many Germans were there on their way to Rotterdam in a starving condition, and asked assistance to help support them, they being unable to do so by themselves. In a long and very polite letter dated on the 26th of August, the Rotterdammers replied, and went into the details of what they had already done for those who had come among them, and how they had at great expense adopted precautions to prevent the arrival of any more. They told the Brielle people that but for these precautions, the general situation would be still worse.

On September 16th, 1709, the Burgomasters of Rotterdam again met in council, and a letter from the English Minister Dayrolles was read, in which he requested that the city should order that no more Germans should be sent or allowed to go to England. The wily Hollanders in reply made answer that "they could not prevent those families of the Palatines who were already in this country in order to go to England, from being taken thither, but that the Minister at Cologne and Frankfurt should be ordered to warn the people over there not to come this way for that purpose," and that is all the satisfaction Minister Dayrolles got. Finally, the city of Rotterdam prohibited all these emigrants from coming into that place.

It does not appear from any of the records that the Holland Government itself made any appropriations for the maintenance of these people while in that country, but left that duty upon the shoulders of the several municipalities themselves and to the charity of the people at large. No doubt it proved as grievous a burden there, as it did in England when they reached that country. From all the evidence, it appears that the English government was in every case compelled to pay the cost of transportation from Holland to London.

Most opportunely, through the liberality of the Pennsylvania Historical Society, new and original records have been thrown open to our inspection and use, in a copy of the original Board of Trade Journals which that Society has had made, and in which are recorded the " Proceedings of her Majesty's Commissioners for promoting the trade of this Kingdom and for inspecting and improving her Plantations in America and elsewhere." The notice of the Commissioners was first called to this question by a letter from the Earl of Sunderland, on May 4, 1709, who was Secretary of State at the time, who stated that some hundreds of poor German Protestants had lately arrived, that more were coming, and asking the Board to consider the best means of settling them in some part of the kingdom.

In all, I find that the Board met about twenty times to consider the various phases presented by the German exodus. All the action that was taken by the Government seems to have been inspired by the discussions and investigations of the Commissioners. The task before the Commissioners was a troublesome one and took up much of their time during the summer of 1709.[12a]

[12a] See Appendix B.

CAUSES LEADING TO THE EXODUS.

THE QUESTION OF PERSECUTION EXAMINED—E N G L A N D's
SHARE IN THE WORK—THE COLD WINTER OF 1708-1709—
OPERATIONS OF THE LAND COMPANIES—PENN'S INVITA-
TIONS—LETTERS FROM PENNSYLVANIA AND BOOKLETS.

ROYAL ARMS OF HOLLAND.

SO remarkable was this Palatine emigration that historians have endeavored to discover some great moving cause, some all powerful impulse to which they might ascribe it. They have not found it for it did not exist. After going over the ground carefully, however, I have had no difficulty in reaching very convincing and satisfactory conclusions.

No single cause was responsible for this wonderful exodus of a people from their firesides, who, perhaps, beyond all others, are most strongly attached to home and country. There was probably since the fall of the Roman Empire, no period of greater unrest in Europe than the closing years of the seventeenth and the opening years of the eighteenth century. The ceaseless disturber of the world's peace, the arch plotter of Europe was still alive, and although past seventy years of age, Louis XIV continued to keep almost every country within his reach, embroiled in foreign or domestic strife. For forty years he had been almost continuously at war with foreign powers. The war of the Spanish succession was now on. Spain, Italy, Germany and the Netherlands echoed to the tramp of desolating armies. Peter the Great and his allies, the kings of Denmark and Poland, were struggling with Charles XII of Sweden, and the contest convulsed the North and East of Europe for more than twenty years.

Germany had for many years been the battle field of Europe. The soldiers of almost every nation had in turn trampled on her soil and despoiled her people. The Palatinate, bordering both on France and Germany had been the provinces most subject to invasion and spoliation. Surely, this dreadful condition of things was in itself enough to induce these miserable people to forsake the land of their birth by thousands.

RELIGIOUS PERSECUTIONS.

So far as I have been able to learn there were at this time no direct religious persecutions; the testimony on this point is concurrent and conclusive. But there were men still living who remembered the days of old; whose friends and relatives had passed through the tortures of the stake and the fagot, and who would carry those memories to their dying day. There are extant two long letters,[13] written in 1698, in which the religious condition of the Protestant Palatines is fully described. They give in detail the broken promises and petty persecutions of the Elector. How the treaty of Munster was shamelessly ignored. We know that religious motives sent the Puritans and the Quakers to the New World, and this had also much to do in setting on foot the Teutonic emigration that turned towards Pennsylvania. By the treaty of Westphalia, only three confessions were tolerated in Germany: the Catholic, Reformed and Lutheran. The "sect" people passed under the yoke.[14] It was that which sent the Mennonites, the Schwenckfelders and the Mystics of Ephrata and the Wissahicon to Pennsylvania. This fact crops out on every page of their history. Whenever contemporary authorities deal with this German exodus, the religious aspect of the case is invariably introduced and frequently is the only one alluded to. We must not forget, however, that whether the emigrants left the Fatherland in larger or smaller numbers, there were nearly always some Catholics among them. In the great migration under consideration

---

[13] "A true account of the sad condition of the Protestants in the Palatinate, in 1698, in two letters to an English gentleman." These letters were originally printed in London in 1699, by Richard Parker.

[14] Seidensticker.

the Catholics were quite numerous. Many of these who refused to embrace the Protestant religion, were sent back to the Palatinate where the ruling house, as well as the ruling prince, as has already been said, were both Catholic. While, therefore, the questions of persecution and religious motives are to be considered, they were by no means the only, not even the principal ones. It is true that in a memorial which was issued in their behalf in London, there are allusions to persecutions, but these occurred full twenty years before.

The Elector, John William, seems to have been stung by the oft-repeated charge of having persecuted his Protestant subject, and in consequence, the Protestant Consistory of the Palatinate, by his direction, issued and spread throughout Britain, Holland and Germany, the following declaration:

"Good Queen Anne," as her own and succeeding generations have delighted to call her, Queen of Great Britain and the last sovereign of the House of Stuart, was born on Feb. 6th, 1665. She was the daughter of the Duke of York, afterwards James II of England, and VII of Scotland. Although her father embraced the Catholic religion, Anne, who had been educated in the Protestant faith, always retained an ardent affection for it. She married Prince George of Denmark in 1683, an indolent but good natured sort of a man. On the death of William III, she succeeded to the crown. During the earlier part of her reign, she was largely under the influence of the Duke of Marlborough and his scheming wife, and this was manifested in much of her public career. Party strife ran high and political combinations made her reign a turbulent one. The successes of that great Captain, the Duke of Marlborough, made her reign a continual scene of public glory. The Union of Scotland with the British crown was consummated while she occupied the throne. So many eminent men in literature and science flourished at this time, that her's has been called the Augustan age of Britain.

A Translation from the High-Dutch, *of a Declaration made (by Direction from the* Elector Palatine) *by the Protestant Consistory in the* Palatinate.

"WHereas it has been signify'd to the Re-
" form'd Consistory in the *Palatinate,*that
" several of the Families, who are gone down the
" *Rhine,* to proceed to *Pensilvania,* to settle them-
" selves there, commonly pretend they are ob-
" lig'd to retire thither for the Sake of Religion,
" and the Persecution which they suffer upon that
" Account; and since it is not known to any of
" the Consistory, that those with-drawn Subjects
" have complain'd, that they suffer'd at that
" Time any Persecution on Account of Religi-
" on, or that they were forc'd to quit their
" Country for want of Liberty of Conscience, con-
" trary to his Electoral Highness's gracious Decla-
" tion of the 21st of *November,* 1705. therefore, as
" soon as the Consistory understood that a Num-
" ber of Subjects were gone out Abroad to the said
" *Pensilvania,* and that more were like to follow,
" they thought it necessary to acquaint all the
" reform'd Inspectors and Ministers with it, to
" undeceive their Auditors, as also these with-
" drawn Peeple, and that they are not like to gain
" their End in all Probability, and to perswade
" them against their withdrawing any farther;
" as also to the Intent to shew the groundless Pre-
" tences of such Peeple to go out of the Country
" on Account of the said Religious Persecution.
" Which we do attest hereby in favour of Truth.
" Done at *Heidleburg* the 27th of *June,* 1709.
  " *L. S.* The Vice-President and Council of the
" Consistory constituted in the Electoral *Palatinate.*
  " *V. P. Howmuller, T. Heyles, H. Croutz, J. Closter.
                           Z. Kirchmejer. Schemal.*

If it were possible to ascertain with fullness and certainty, the extent to which Queen Anne and her government were responsible for this movement, I am fully satisfied we had about reached the true solution. England retained a lively remembrance of the results that followed the revocation of the Edict of Nantes. That unwise act sent 700,000 of France's best citizens to Germany, Switzerland, Holland and Britain. They were largely handicraftsmen and carried their various manufacturing industries, their skill and their industry with them, giving thereby a wonderful impulse to industrial trades wherever they went. The long and costly wars England had carried on, took away many of her people and this was felt to be a most serious drawback to national prosperity. It was desirable to replace them with the unsatisfied people of Germany, who were known to be skillful in many trades, as well as reliable and thrifty.

I have found a number of references to a proclamation by the Queen, said to favor, if not actually invite, these people to come to England.[14a] A careful

---

Queen Anne was too much swayed by her ministers and favorites to be called a great Queen, but as a woman she deserves our admiration. She was a sincere friend of the Palatines, doing everything in her power to improve their condition while in England, and to settle them comfortably elsewhere. She was of medium size, comely, but not beautiful. If she was not great as a queen, never was there a more virtuous, affectionate and conscientious a woman or one more worthy of esteem. Our portrait is a reproduction from the famous one of Sir Godfrey Kneller.

[14a] ' On a proclamation of Queen Anne, of England, 1708, some three

examination of all the authorities that were accessible to me, shows no evidence sustaining this allegation. There is no reason to suspect her of even having authorized the famous "Golden Book," so largely circulated in Germany, containing a portrait of herself, with the title printed in gold. That she was throughout these trying times the sincere friend of these immigrants, there is no room to doubt. We are told in Luttrell's diary that in response to a letter from the King of Prussia, she declared she had already given her ministers abroad, instructions to aid the French Protestants and would further aid them as far as lay in her power. The fact is that her treatment of them while in England was everything that could reasonably be expected of her, and that she even sent assistance to those in Holland, clearly shows that the earnest sympathies of the warm hearted Queen were thoroughly aroused in the cause of these homeless wanderers. If any proclamation had been issued by her, it would surely be in

---

or four thousand Germans went in 1709, to Holland, and were thence transported to England." Rupp's Hist. Lancaster county, p. 182.

Löehr says : Da verzweifelten viele am Leben, *und als die Einladung der englischen Königin Anna*, eine freie Uberfahrt nach Amerika, und gutes Land umsonst zu gewinnen, den Rhein entlang verkundigt wurde, brach man in Masse auf, und es begab sich jener Zug der mehr als dreiszig tausand Deutchen, welcher ein Denkmal ist des deutchen Elends." *Die Deutchen in Amerika, p. 42.*

Rupp evidently followed Löehr blindly as others have done since. If these writers have any evidence of what they assert why have they not produced it, or indicated chapter and verse where it may be found? I reiterate therefore that I am fully persuaded the story is a mere figment of the imagination, having its origin in the Queen's well-known kindly attitude towards these people.

Drawn by J. Thurston.

Engraved by R. Rivers.

SIDNEY GODOLPHIN.

Lord High Treasurer of Great Britain from 1702
until 1710.

*From a Drawing by Bulfinch in the Collection
at Strawberry Hill.*

evidence somewhere. But even the inquiry insti-
gated by the House of Commons as to the causes of
this influx of Palatines, and undertaken by an oppo-
site administration, failed to reveal anything of the
kind. Surely if there had been such a thing, it
would have been discovered. I am fully satisfied
therefore, that no such document was ever issued,
either by the Government or by the Queen. It was
simply one way of accounting for a perplexing condition of things.[14b]

THE COLD WINTER OF 1708-9.

I am inclined to believe that a most potent cause
in bringing about this remarkable migration was the
cold winter of 1708-9. All the contemporary author-

[14b] The Ministry at this period was Whig. Charles Spencer, Earl of
Sunderland was Secretary of State, from 1706 until 1710; and Sidney,
Earl of Godolphin, was Lord High Treasurer, from 1702 until 1710. In
the latter year, however, there was a change in the political complexion
of the country. The Tories came into power, with Henry St. John,
Viscount Bolingbroke, as Foreign Secretary, and Robert Harley, Earl
of Oxford, as Chancellor of the Exchequer. The German immigration
having been most distasteful to the majority of the English people,
especially the lower classes, the new Ministry at once proceeded to make
itself popular by beginning an inquiry into the causes of the coming of so
many thousands of these people. A parliamentary committee consisting
of sixty-nine members of the House was appointed to make a searching
investigation "upon what invitation or encouragement the Palatines
came over and what moneys were expended in bringing them into
Great Britain, and for maintaining them here, and by whom paid,"
but nothing was discovered incriminating the former administration, or
connecting the Queen with the movement except in a way to do her ex-
ceeding honor. This investigation was a fortunate thing, inasmuch
as it has made us acquainted with much concerning this movement
which otherwise might never have been disclosed.

ities are agreed as to its unexampled severity. It was general throughout Western Europe, but especially was it felt among the starving citizens of the Palatinate, whose lands and homes had so long and so often been despoiled by persecutions and wars. The pen almost refuses to do its task when asked to tell of the hundreds of strong men who, during that memorable winter, lay down to die of cold and hunger in the once fruitful valley of the Rhine. So intense was the cold that even the wild animals of the forest and the birds of the air were frozen to death. Wine was frozen in the casks and bottles. The vineyards were frozen to the ground and the fruit trees completely destroyed.[15]

Tindal refers to the intense frost of that winter. He says: "The severity of the winter season was very remarkable this year, (1708-9), for it began to freeze the night before Christmas Day, with great violence, and not long after fell great snows. Those who compared the great frost of 1683-4 with this, observed that the first was generally a bright one, and continued about two months without interruption; but the latter mostly dark, with some intervals lasted a month longer; during which many cattle, especially sheep, and likewise birds, perished. The Thames was frozen over, and on the 3rd of January, people began to erect booths and set up tents on the ice. This occasioned a thin harvest and

---

[15] See Löehr, who says: "Endlich kam der gräszliche Winter von 1709, hinzu, wo die Vögel in der Luft und das Wild in den Wäldern erfroren und die Menchen verhungerten. Page 42.

this a scarcity of corn. This great frost was general in Europe, but most severely felt in France, where in most places the fruit trees were killed, and the corn frozen to the ground, which occasioned there a dreadful calamity and desolation."[16]

Need we wonder, therefore, that these wretched people, who had previously undergone so much from the invasions of contending armies, were at length driven to despair by this terrible visitation of the forces of nature? Where armies were no longer able to collect resources, what hope was there for the individual citizen? Their heart-rending lamentations filled the listening air and existence seemed only possible in another clime and under new conditions. To make matters worse, even in that time of dire distress, speculators came to the front, bought the grain that frugal farmers had saved and sought to make a profit even out of famine. Nor could all the efforts on the part of the government check it. An eye witness says of the financial situation: "Nobody could pay any more, because nobody was paid. The people of the country in consequence of exactions had become insolvent; commerce dried up and brought no returns. Good faith and confidence were abolished." Chaos, ruin and universal suffering prevailed.

I come now to what, after all, may be ascribed the principal cause leading up to this extraordinary

---

[16] Tindal's History of England, Book xxvi. See also James' History of Louis XIV.

movement. William Penn had made two visits to Germany, one in 1671 and the second in 1677. At that time he had not yet acquired the Province that was to make his name so memorable. But he became well known through the peculiar religious tenets he advocated and attempted to spread. Later, when the owner of Pennsylvania, he spared no efforts to attract colonists from Germany. Not only did he write full descriptions of the Province where lands were almost given away, but political and religious toleration was proclaimed as the very corner stone of his new government. Many of these attractively written brochures are still extant to show us how great were the efforts to arouse the spirit of emigration.

Then, too, the spirit of speculation stepped in and did much to forward the project. One company after another was formed to arouse and encourage the migrating impulse. The West India Company, The Frankford Company and many more were engaged in this work. Seidensticker tells us that the latter company is directly attributable to Penn. He also asserts that Penn gave the first impulse to this German exodus.[17] Bancroft bears testimony to the same effect.[18] The climate, resources and general advantages of Penn's Province were well known all over Germany.

It is true that more than a generation had passed

[17] Der anstosz zur deutchen Auswanderung im eigentlichen Sinne ging von William Penn aus. Bilder, p. 4.

Groß-
Brittannisches
AMERICA

Nach seiner
Erfindung/Bevölckerung
und
Allerneuestem Zustand.

Terre-Neuf.	St. Lucia.
Neu-Schottländ.	St. Vincent.
Neu-Engelland.	Dominico.
Neu-Yorck.	Antego.
Neu-Jersey.	Montserrat.
Pensylvanien.	Nevis.
Maryland.	Barbuda.
Virginien.	Anguilla.
Carolina.	Jamaica.
Hudsons-Bay.	Bahama/ und
Barbados.	Bermudas.

Aus dem Englischen übersetzt
durch
M. Vischer.

Hamburg/ in Verlegung Zacharias Hertels
Buchhändlers im Dohm/ 1710.

TITLE PAGE OF GERMAN EDITION OF OLDMIXON'S BRITISH
AMERICA.

by since the gentle Quaker's, visit to the Rhine provinces, and many of those who had met him face to
face were no longer among the living. But there were
still some there who had seen and heard him. A new
series of publications also began to appear about the
year 1700, and these were widely distributed all over
Germany and the Low Countries. Once more the
tales of a land flowing with milk and honey were
told ; a land where the climate was more temperate
than in Germany ; where the conditions of life were
most desirable ; where all creeds were tolerated ;
where kings and priestcraft were unknown ; where
universal freedom prevailed ; where strife never
came ; where not only ease and comfort but certain
wealth awaited the industrious settlers :—this and
much more was heard around every fireside and fell
like the voice of enchantment upon the ears of the
harried and starving Palatines. There was also an
old German prophecy to the effect that in America
they would prosper and be happy.[19] With all these
things continually pressed upon their attention, and
with the grim spectre of spoliations, hardships, in-
tolerance and want rising gloomily out of the past,
need we seek further, need we even wonder, that

---

[18] "Meanwhile the news spread abroad that William Penn, the
Quaker, had opened 'an asylum to the good and the oppressed of every
nation,' and humanity went through Europe, gathering the children of
misfortune. From England and Wales, from Scotland and Ireland and
the Low Countries emigrants crowded to the land of promise."
Bancroft's United States, vol. 2, p. 391.

[19] E. K. Martin. The Mennonites.

entire communities uprose as one man, shook the dust of the Fatherland from their feet—that Fatherland so dear to the German heart—and with little or no preparation, took flight for a land where their lives should thereafter be passed in plenty and in peace?

Another cause and by no means an unimportant one must also be mentioned. The colonists who had come to Pennsylvania prior to 1709, were, with very few exceptions, satisfied with the condition of things as they found them. The Germantown colony itself was in the land business, and therefore interested in bringing over as many colonists as possible. Selfish motives may have moved the people of Germantown equally with their desire to benefit their countrymen, but whatever the motive, it turned the expectant eyes and the waiting footsteps towards the New World.

BRITAIN'S NATURALIZATION ACT.

Still another cause remains to be mentioned. For twenty years the passage of a general naturalization law for Protestant foreigners coming into, or residing in the Kingdom, conditioned on their taking the oaths and communing in the English church, had been discussed in the newspapers and by pamphleteers. Up to this time Holland had drawn to herself most of the German Protestants who had emigrated from Catholic states, enriching that country by their industries and their thrift. Englishmen were anxious to turn at least a portion of these people across the channel. This eventually led to the passage of the naturalization law.[20] Luttrell thought this matter so important that he gave it close attention in his diary as the following will show :

Saturday, Feb. 5, 1709. The Commons this day gave leave to bring in a bill for naturalizing all foreign protestants.

Thursday, Feb. 24. This day a second time the bill for naturalizing foreign protestants, and committed it for Monday.

Tuesday, 1 March. Yesterday the Commons in a Committee, went through the bill for naturalizing foreign protestants, and to be repeated to-morrow.

Thursday, 3 March. The Commons ordered the bill for naturalizing foreign protestants to be engrost.

Thursday, March 24. Yesterday the Lords Commissioners appointed by her Majesty, sent for the Commons to come up to the House of Peers, and gave the royal assent to the bill for naturalizing protestants.

Saturday, 14 May. A great many poor German and French protestants have taken the oaths this

---

[20] An extract from the oath which these naturalized foreigners were compelled to take, is here given :

Ich, A. B. schwere, dass ich von ganzem Herzen verabscheue und abschwere, als gottlos und ketzerisch, die verdammte Lehre und Satz, dass Fürsten, welche der PAPST, oder der Romische Stuhl, hat in Bann gethan, können von ihren Unterthanen, oder sonst jemanden, abgesetzt und ermordet werden. Und ich bekenne, dass kein ausländischer Fürst, Person, Prälat, Stand order Potentat habe, oder soll haben, einige Jurisdiction, Gewalt, Oberherrschaft, Vorzug, oder Autorität in Geistlichen und Kirchen-Sachen in diesem Königreich. So helfe mir Gott.

CHARLES *Earl of* SUNDERLAND.

Secretary of State of Great Britain from 1706
until 1710.

week at the Queen's Bench Court, in order to their naturalization by the late act.[20a]

While the act was passed about the time the first emigrants began to arrive, and would therefore not seem to have been an inducing cause, yet the concurrent testimony of a number of authorities on this point seems nevertheless to give color to this fact.

One authority say: "In consequence of the naturalization act, there came over in May, 7000 of the poor Palatines and Swabians, who had been utterly ruined and driven from their habitations by the French.[21] Dick Steele, when the immigration had set in, said in the *Tatler:* " Our late act of naturalization hath had so great effect in foreign parts, that some princes have prohibited the French refugees in their dominions to sell or transfer their estates to any other of their subjects; and at the same time have granted them greater immunities than they hitherto enjoyed. It has been also thought necessary to restrain their own subjects from leaving their country on pain of death.[22] The latter clause no doubt refers to the Elector Palatine himself, as Luttrell under date of April 28, says: "Foreign letters advise that the Elector Palatine, upon many families leaving his dominions and gone to England to be transported to Pennsylvania, has published an order making it death and confiscation of goods, for any of his sub-

---

[20a] A Brief Historical Relation of State Affairs from Sept. 1678 to April, 1714. By Narcissus Luttrell, Oxford, 1857. 6 vols.

[21] Anderson's History of England.

[21] Tatler, No. 13, May, 1709.

jects to quit their native countries."[23]   It must be con-
fessed, that cause and effect in this case seem to follow each other very closely, but no doubt it was well
known that the law would be passed and men made
ready in anticipation.   Holland, too, seems to have
thought the act had something to do with the great
outgoing of the people, as on the 24th of June, just
three months after the English law was promulgated,
the States General issued a proclamation, offering to
naturalize all the refugees from France and other
countries who had sought a domicile in Holland, and
confer on them and all other worthy persons who
might hereafter come, all the privileges of citizenship.[23a]

While various accounts, among them those set
forth by the Palatines themselves after they arrived
in England, give various reasons for this extraordinary movement, yet through them all runs one long,
unvarying refrain—the hope of bettering themselves,
of securing religious toleration and domestic tran-
quillity.   I say again, therefore, as I have already
said, that no one reason or cause was responsible for
this remarkable movement, but that it was the result
of a combination of causes, which had long been at
work, and which at length made themselves seen
and felt in the manner here set forth.

---

[23] Luttrell's Diary.
[23a] See Appendix D.

THE STAY IN ENGLAND.

MAINTAINED BY GOVERNMENT AID AND BY PRIVATE SUB-
SCRIPTIONS—VARIOUS PROJECTS FOR THEIR SETTLEMENT—
SCATTERED IN ALL PARTS OF THE KINGDOM—UNHAPPY
CONDITION AND THEIR APPEAL TO THE PUBLIC—INCIDENTS
OF THEIR LIFE IN LONDON.

Arms of Penn.

WE now come to the long stay of these Palatines in London and the surrounding country, a stay that was not more agreeable to them than it was unwelcome to the English. Never before, p e r h a p s, were emigrants seeking new homes in a distant land, so poorly provided with money and the other necessaries of life to support them on their way, as were these Palatines. All contemporary accounts agree on this point and there is besides abundant evidence to sustain them.

Ships had to be provided by the English govern-

ment to bring them from Rotterdam. From the day
of their arrival in London they required the assistance of the English to keep them from starving.
There was little or no work ; bread was dear, and the
only thing to do was to bridge the crisis by raising
money by public subscriptions. On June 7, 1709, the
Justices of the Peace for the county of Middlesex,
sent a petition to the Queen, asking for authority to
take up collections in their behalf in all the churches,
as well as from the public generally, throughout the
county. The Queen not only granted the desired
authority, but on June 16, in Council, she being
present, orders were prepared and a Brief was issued
at once. This Brief was soon thereafter made to extend to the entire kingdom, including Scotland and
Wales, the need having grown from day to day, and
the charge on the crown having become a burden. In
this paper recital was made of the many hardships
these people had suffered in their own country during
the previous years, and it was ordered that collections
should be lifted in all the churches, and that the
curates and wardens should proceed from house to
house, asking for contributions which were to be distributed among the needy Palatines through a Royal
Commission, which included the Archbishop of Canterbury, the Lord High Chancellor, the Dukes of
Devonshire, Newcastle, Somerset, Ormond, Bedford,
and Buckingham, besides many of the most eminent
persons among the gentry.[24]

The well known Bishop Burnet, who throughout
these troublesome times was the staunch friend of

the Palatines, at the same time sent out a circular letter to the clergy of his diocese, asking their earnest efforts to stir up the people to be liberal in this charity. The result of these efforts was that the large sum of £19,838.11 was collected and distributed to relieve their necessities. Considering the difference in the value of money between that period and the present time, it must be admitted the Englishmen were liberal, especially when we remember how long wars, and the payment of subsidies to other nations, absorbed the money of the English nation. At that very hour, the King of Denmark, the King of Portugal, the Duke of Savoy, the King of Prussia, the Landgrave of Hesse Cassel, the Elector of Treves and the Elector Palatine were all heavily subsidized by the English Government, on account of the war then carried on.

But while food was thus provided, shelter was also needed. The Queen directed that a thousand tents be taken out of the Tower of London for their use. But of course these were far from sufficient, and for a time even no suitable place to pitch them could be found. Eventually, part were set up on Blackheath,[25]

---

[24] In Appendix C will be found the full text of the petition sent to the Queen by the Justices of the Peace for the county of Middlesex, as well as the "Brief" issued by the Queen in response to the same. A full list of the persons who were appointed to superintend these collections is also appended as a matter of historic interest. One hundred persons were engaged in the work.

[25] Blackheath was a large, elevated, open common in the county of Kent, seven miles south-east of London. Once it was of considerable size but it has been encroached upon to such an extent that at present it

on the south side of the Thames, near Greenwich, and the rest at Camberwell.[26] Some found lodgings in private houses, others were permitted to occupy barns until harvest time, when, of course they would be required to house the crops. Sir Charles Cox gave up his large warehouse, although desired by the parish officers not to do so, for fear of the expense and of probable infection. He offered it for two

---

comprises only about 70 acres. For several hundred years it has been a favorite holiday resort of the citizens of London. The inimitable diarist Samuel Pepys, speaks of having gone there in 1665 to test a carriage fitted with springs, a new invention, it would seem. This high-lying spot was also a favorite military camping ground. John Evelyn says, under date of June 10, 1673, 'we went, after dinner, to see the formal and formidable camp on Blackheath, raised to invade Holland; or, as others suspected, for another design." In 1683 he visited the same spot to see "the new fair," it pretended to be for the sale of cattle he tells us, but adds, "There appeared nothing but an innumerable assembly of people from London, peddlers, &c." Again in 1685 he was there to see six Scotch and English regiments encamped there, about to return to Holland: "The King and Queen came to see them exercise." The last visit he records was made on July 20, 1690, on which day, "a camp of about 4,000 men was begun to be formed on Blackheath."

Blackheath is also noted for being the scene of some of the most important occurrences in the English history. The peasant revolt under Wat Tyler originated there. Jack Cade, the leader of the insurrection of 1450, when he marched on London with upwards of 15,000 adherents, encamped on this historic spot. The revolutionary Cornishmen under Lord Audley in 1497 also made it their stopping place. The Danes, at the time of their invasion of Britain, in 1011, encamped here. To this renowned place flocked all London to welcome Henry V. upon his return to England after winning the glorious field of Agincourt. Here also, Charles II, on his way from Dover met the army of the Restoration. Blackheath, even so late as the closing years of the eighteenth century was a famous resort of highwaymen and some of the most notorious cut-purses in England's criminal annals made it the scene of their exploits. [See Evelyn's Diary: Chambers Encyclopædia, etc.]

[26] Camberwell was, and is a parish and suburb of London, in the county of Surry, distant about two miles from St. Paul's Cathedral.

months without rent, but conditioned that if they remained longer he was to be paid for the entire time. He was paid 100 guineas to allow them to remain until they were sent to Ireland and elsewhere. He received that sum on Feb. 9, 1710. Fourteen hundred were lodged there.

Meanwhile the Board of Trade, which had the general supervision of the whole business, was not idle. The records of this Board, which have been rendered accessible during the past few months in this country, give ample testimony to the trouble and anxiety these people were causing the Government.[26a] It met almost daily in the palace of Whitehall and from the proceedings we get a clear idea of what was done to support and establish them.[27]

[26a] See Appendix B.

[27] The historian, Macaulay, calls Whitehall "the most celebrated palace in which the Eng ish sovereigns have ever dwelt." It once occupied an area of great extent, fronting the Thames on the east, St James Park on the west and stretching from Scotland Yard on the north to Cannon-row on the south. If the walls of this venerable structure could record the sayings and doings they have heard and witnessed, the chronicle would almost fill up the mediæval history of England. From the days of the Tudors to those of the Stuarts, the names of the most illustrious personages in the history of the empire have been closely associated with this famous place

Its original name was York House, so named by Cardinal Wolsey, who once lived in it, but when that proud prelate lost the favor of his Sovereign, it was surrendered to the crown, when it received its present name. It was the palace of the Kings of England from the reign of Henry VIII, to William III. There was at one time a thoroughfare through it to St. Margaret's cemetery which offended King Henry VIII, so he opened a new burying ground at St. Martin's-in-the-Fields. In front of the banqueting hall of the palace, on January 30, 1649, was enacted one of the darkest scenes in all English history, the execution on the scaffold of Charles I.

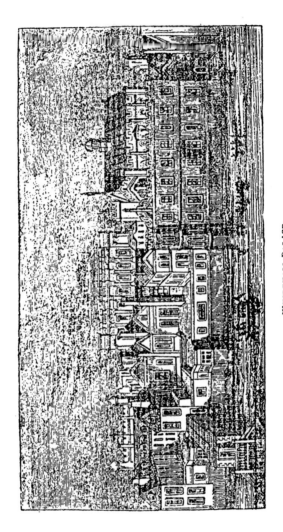

WHITEHALL PALACE.

Several times it was proposed to locate them in different parts of the kingdom itself. They called to their assistance the Lutheran and Reformed clergymen in London, three in number, at the time, who it seems were located in the Savoy district,[28] and

In addition to being the Royal residence, Whitehall was also the place where all the public officials of the Kingdom had their offices. The Treasury, the offices of the Privy Council, of the Secretary of State, of the Lords of the Board of Trade, and indeed all the important public departments were located here. It was in the rooms of the Board of Commissioners for the Colonies that all the discussions concerning the Palatines were carried on, as will be seen by a reference to Appendix B. It is this fact that gives us a direct interest in this famous building and has led me to introduce a pictorial illustration of it in this connection.

On January 4, 1698, a most disastrous fire broke out in the Palace lasting all night, and by morning some of the most notable parts of the structure had been swept away. Many masterpieces of art and other treasures were destroyed. Macaulay devotes several pages in Chap. xxiii of his History to this occurrence

[28] The "SAVOY" is a well known district in London. The "Savoy Palace" was built here by Peter of Savoy in the first part of the XIV century. It was the scene of many stirring events in English history. It was destroyed by Wat Tyler and his fellow rebels in 1381. Henry VII rebuilt it and endowed it as a hospital. King Charles I established a French church there. Fleetwood describes it in 1581 as "the chief nurserie of evil people, rogues and masterless men," it having become a refuge for poor debtors when fleeing from their creditors. The *London Postman* of 1696 says "a person going into the Savoy to collect a debt due him was seized by the inhabitants and according to usual custom, dipped in tar and rolled in feathers." In 1661 the Commission appointed to revise the Book of Common Prayer met here, and was known as the Savoy Conference.

In 1694 a German Lutheran congregation was established in the Savoy district and met in the Savoy chapel. It is this church, known as St. Mary's of Savoy and the clergymen who ministered therein in 1709 to which allusion is made above. At this period there seem to have been three clergymen there ; George Andreas Ruperti. Mr. Tribekko and (perhaps) Mr. Treke. These were the persons who seem also to have had general charge of the newly arrived Germans. It was here that their spiritual

THE SAVOY PALACE AND CHAPEL.

these, from time to time, every few days in fact, made
reports of the numbers of the Palatines, their con-

---

home was and here the ministrations of the church were given them.
Here the sacraments were administered and here, when they died, as
many hundreds did, the last rites were performed and they were laid to
rest in the burial ground belonging to the church.   It is a "God's acre"
to which the men of German blood, wherever they may be, will
always turn with feelings of profound interest and reverence.

A German Reformed congregation was also established within the
bounds of the Savoy district, about the year 1697.   One of its earliest pastors was the Rev. Planta, who was also the Chief Librarian of the British
Museum, and Secretary of the Royal Academy of Sciences.   A few
years later the Congregation was in charge of the Rev. Dr. Gottfried
Woide, who also became Chief Librarian of the British Museum.

dition, needs, and occupations.[29] It was stated that most of the men were husbandmen, and many of the rest handcraftsmen, while the women could spin and knit. The first 852 were allowed £20 per day. It was also proposed that they be granted parcels of land in her Majesty's forests and chases in order to convert them to tillage. A proposition was also received from the Society of London for Mines Royal, proposing the employment of the strongest in the silver and copper mines of Penlyn and Merionethshire. A project for settling some of them in Staffordshire and Gloucestershire, proposed by Lord Chamberlain, was also considered. Eventually it was found this would entail a cost of £150,000 and it was abandoned. It was suggested to employ some of them in the mines of Wales. It was agreed, however, to give special encouragement to persons and parishes who should be willing to receive them, and the sum of £5 was offered per head, the Queen to be at the charge of sending them to their respective places.

Still the allowance of the government was insufficient to properly sustain these people, and they were obliged to beg for bread on the streets of London, and this begging was principally done by the married women.

A contemporary publication in summing up these events said : " Some well meaning but perhaps not sufficiently thoughtful persons, touched by the suffer-

---

[29] See Appendix B.

KIRCHEN-
ORDNUNG,

DerChriftlichen und der ungeänderten
Augfpurgifchen Confeffion
Zugethanen
Gemeinde in LONDON,

Welche,
Durch Gottliche Verleyhung,
Im 1694. Jahre,
An 19ten *Sonntage nach dem Feft der Heiligen*
Dreyfaltigkeit,
Solenniter Eingeweyhet und Eingefegnet
worden,

In St. Mary's Savoy.

Ep. 1. Cor. 14. v. 33. 40.
GOTT *ift nicht ein* GOTT *der Unordnung, fondern des*
Friedens, wie in allen Gemeinen der Heiligen. Laffe
es alles ehrlich und ordentlich zugehen.
Rom. 15. v. 33.
Der GOTT *des Friedens fey mit euch allen! Amen.*

TITLE PAGE OF PRAYER-BOOK OF THE GERMAN SAVOY
CONGREGATION IN LONDON. USED IN
PENNSYLVANIA PRIOR TO 1748.

ings of the Palatines, ruined through long wars and heavy taxes, had allowed themselves to be informed that these people could be better cared for in England if they betook themselves thither, and from thence to places to be indicated. This resulted in a great uprising in the Palatinate and the adjoining regions, so that the people hastened to England in great numbers, hoping to find there long desired happiness and abundance of food, and in a short time many thousands reached English soil, so that in May, 6520 persons had arrived. It had been the intention to provide for all of these in the Province of Kent, negotiations had been begun to purchase the large forest and zoological garden at Coloham, belonging to Sir Joseph Williamson, and which had been offered for sale, but he declined to sell it although offered its full value according to the estimates of the day. Meanwhile the poor people lay there and more were almost daily added to their number. Germany was notified that no more could be received, and several hundred Catholics were sent back with alms, because they could not be allowed to remain under the laws of the realm. For the remainder huts were built and a number of dwelling places in Hampshire allotted them to live in. One hundred commissioners,[30] representing all ranks and conditions, were appointed, among them dukes, margraves, earls, bishops and others, and a collection throughout the entire kingdom was permitted for

---

[30] For complete list of the names see Appendix C.

their benefit, which must have produced a large sum, because some persons contributed 500 thalers and others even 1000, and the Queen herself ordered a daily distribution of 800 thalers among them, and also gave them 1000 High-German Bibles."[31]

From the beginning they were objects of dislike by the poorer classes of the English people. It was said they came to eat the bread of Englishmen and reduce the scale of wages; the latter, it was alleged, had already fallen from 18 pence to 15 pence where they were encamped. "It was also charged that they retained their love of their native land, corresponded with their friends in Germany and might act as spies, and eventually might even destroy the true British character of the race." These representations excited a rancorous prejudice against these unfortunates. To many Englishmen the name of German was synonymous with that of Roman Catholic. Hence the dislike and distrust with which the majority of the lower ranks among the English regarded these people. The Tories refused to employ or relieve any except such as were Protestants, and willing to become members of the Church of England. The French refugees who had settled there and who had themselves fled from persecution, are said to have been the most pitiless and jealous of all.[32]

---

[31] The "Theatrum Europaeum."

[32] Cassell's England. Geschichte und Zustanden, p. 43. Geschichsblätter, p. 24.

JOANNES BARO DE CHURCHILL,
DUX et COMES
DE MARLBOROUGH, ℥ ℥ ℥

Ger. la Droon sculp.

To many Englishmen, especially among the lower orders, the name of German was synonymous with that of Roman Catholic, and this fact served to intensify the dislike with which these colonists were regarded upon their arrival in England.

It is hardly to be wondered at, therefore, if the lower classes of Englishmen not only did all they could to drive these Germans out of London, but should resort to actual violence to do so. According to Löher and Kapp, upon one occasion no fewer than 2000 infuriated Englishmen, armed with axes, scythes and smith hammers, made an attack upon one of the German encampments, and struck down all who did not flee. The same writers tell us that at this time there happened to be in London five chiefs of the Mohawk tribe of Indians, who had come to ask the assistance of her Majesty's Government against the attacks of the French in Canada. These, in the course of their wanderings in the neighborhood of London, came upon the Palatine encampment at Blackheath, and seeing their poverty and wretched condition, inquired as to the cause. Being told that the earnest longing of these people was lands in America where they could live and help themselves, they were so moved by what they heard, that they invited the Germans to come to them in America and offered Queen Anne a gift of rich lands whereon they might settle.[33]

---

[33] Löher: Die Deutchen in Amerika, p. 43. See also Hallische Nachrichten, 973-981.

But it was not those in the humbler walks of life
alone who spoke unkindly of these miserable wanderers. Dean Swift had this untruthful fling at them:
" Some persons, whom the voice of the nation
authorizes me to call her enemies, taking advantage
of the general naturalization act, had invited over a
great number of foreigners of all religions, under the
name of Palatines, who understood no trade or handicraft, yet rather chose to beg than labor ; who, besides
infesting our streets, bred contagious diseases by
which we lost in natives thrice the number of population gained in foreigners."[34] In reply to this charge
of the witty, but bitter, dean of St. Patrick's, I may
say I have nowhere discovered any evidence of the
charges he makes concerning an unusual mortality
among the English people, through contact with the
Palatines. If there was any cause whatever, it was
doubtless exaggerated to lend point to the pen of a
caustic Tory writer. It is not to be denied, however,
that insufficient nourishment and exposure had introduced much sickness among them. The report to the
House of Commons on April 14, 1711, of the Committee appointed to consider the petition of the Ministers, Church Wardens and Inhabitants of St.
Olathe, in Southwark, County of Surrey, proves that.
Swift's charge that they understood no trade or
handicraft is wholly untrue, as the numerous lists
made of these people show.[34a] That they did beg is
true, but it was from necessity and not from choice,

<hr>

[34] Examiner, 41, 45.

as a score of authorities fully prove, and none but him deny.

But it must not be supposed that the entire body of the English people were arrayed against these long-suffering wanderers. If they had plenty of enemies they also had some good friends. The great Duke of Marlborough spoke warmly in their favor before the Ministry, during the period of their greatest coming. They were of the race which had filled the ranks of that sturdy champion of Protestantism, Gustavus Adolphus, and Marlborough had himself seen their heroism displayed upon many a stricken field, under his own command. England needed soldiers, and he well knew the world had none better. But no man did the Palatines better service than

---

[34a] "At several Times, from the first of May last past, to the 18th of July 1709, there have been landed in England of these distressed Palatines, the exact Number of 10,000 Souls. Those that arrived at the two first Times, viz : from the first of May, to the 12th of June, consisted of Men having families, 1278 ; Wives, 1234; Widows, 89 ; unmarry'd Men, 384 ; unmarry'd Women, 106 : Boys above 14 Years of Age, 379 ; Girls above 14 Years, 374 ; Boys under 14 Years, 1367 ; Girls under 14 Years, 1309. So that the whole Number of the two first Numbers landed, were 6,520.

Of these, there are Husbandmen and vine dressers, 1083 ; Schoolmasters, 10; Herdsmen, 4 ; Wheelwrights, 13 ; Smiths, 46 ; Cloth and Linnen Weavers, 66 ; Carpenters, 90 ; Bakers. 32 ; Masons, 48 ; Coopers and Brewers, 48 ; Joiners, 20 ; Shoemakers, 40 ; Taylors, 58; Butchers, 15; Millers, 27 ; Sadlers, 7 ; Stocking-weavers, 5 ; Tanners, 7 ; Miners, 3 ; Brick-makers, 6 ; Hatters, 3 ; Hunters, 5 ; Turners, 6; Surgeons, 3 ; Locksmiths, 2 ; Bricklayers, 4 ; Glasiers, 2; Hatters, 3 ; Silver-smiths, 2 ; Carvers, 2 ; 1 Cook and 1 Student. To which above 1500 being added, that arriv'd in the River of Thames, July 18, and others at other Times, whose Families, Trades and Employment, are not yet distinguish'd or number'd, makes the Number of the Palatines amount in the whole to about 10,000 Souls." Palatine Refugees in England, pp. 19-20.

Bishop Burnet.[35] Early and late he was their stead-
fast champion. When the bill to naturalize such as
were willing to take the oath of allegiance, and receive the sacrament in any Protestant Church, came

---

[35] Among the few men of prominence and influence, who during those
trying times resolutely stood up and unselfishly endeavored to meliorate
the condition of these Palatines, the name of Gilbert Burnet, Bishop of
Salisbury, must ever occupy a foremost place. Next to the Queen herself, they seem to have had no better friend.

Burnet was born in Edinburg in 1643. He entered Marischal College,
Aberdeen, at the age of ten. After taking his degree he gave himself
to the study of law, and afterwards to Divinity. He studied Hebrew in
Holland and later became Professor of Divinity in the University of
Glasgow. He resigned his chair and went to London, where he was
made chaplain to the Rolls Chapel. and lecturer at St. Clements. In
1679-81 he published the first two volumes of his History of the Refor-
mation, for which Parliament gave him a vote of thanks. He had sided
with the moderate party and upon his refusal to attach himself to that of
the King, he was deprived of his lectureship. After this he passed to
the continent, travelling in Switzerland, Italy, France and Germany. He
made the acquaintance of the Prince of Orange, with whom he became
a favorite. When William came over to England, Burnet accompanied
him as chaplain and in 1689 was made Bishop of Salisbury. He was of
a disputatious temperament and was involved in many troubles in consequence. He was a voluminous author. He died in 1715 and his
"History of his Own Time " was not published until after his death. In
politics he was a Whig and in consequence was assailed by Swift, Pope
and other Tory writers. He was a broad churchman, sincere in his
views, of strict morality, great charity and moderation, honest and
earnest, but sometimes inclined to be warped in his judgments.

Macaulay devotes several pages of his brilliant history to an analysis
of Burnet's character. He alludes to his many faults of understanding
and temper, but says : "Yet Burnet, though open in many respects to
ridicule, and even to serious censure, was no contemptible man. His
parts were quick, his industry unwearied, his reading various and most
extensive. He was at once a historian, an antiquary, a theologian, a
pamphleteer, a debater and an active political leader ; and in every one
of these he made himself conspicuous among able competitors." The
value of the services of this man to the cause of the poor Palatines,
which he so warmly espoused, can hardly be over-estimated.

Kneller Pinx.

GILBERT BURNET

BISHOP OF SALISBURY

OB, 1714 ·15·

up for action in the House of Lords, many of the ecclesiastical peers demanded that they should take it only in the Established Church, but Bishop Burnet, greatly to the scandal of his brethren, advocated any Protestant form, and carried the day.[36] The Bishop of Chester, a High Churchman, most earnestly opposed such liberal dealing with these foreign Protestants.

ADDRESS OF THE PALATINES.

The Palatines themselves, or some one in their behalf, issued the following address to the English people :

" We, the Poor Distressed *Palatines*, whose utter Ruin was occasioned by the Merciless Cruelty of a Bloody Enemy, the French, whose prevailing Power some Years past, like a torrent, rushed into our Country and overwhelmed us at once ; and being not Content with Money and Food Necessary for their Occasions, not only dispossessed us of all Support but inhumanly burnt our Houses to the Ground, whereby being deprived of all Shelter, we were turned into the open Fields, there with our Families to seek what shelter we could find, were obliged to make the earth our Repository for Rest, and the clouds our Canopy or Covering.

" We poor wretches in this deplorable condition made our Humble Supplication and Cries to Almighty God, whose Omnisciency is extensive, who has promised to relieve all those that make their

---

[36] Cassell's History of England.

Humble Supplications to him that he will hear them; Relieve them and Support them in what Condition soever; and likewise has promised to all those who shall feed the Hungry, Cloath the Naked, and Comfort the Distressed, they shall be received into his Everlasting Kingdom, where they shall be rewarded with Eternal Life.

" We magnify the Goodness of our Great God, who heard our Prayers, and in his good Time disposed the Hearts of Good and Pious Princes to a Christian Compassion and Charity towards us in this deplorable State, by whose Royal Bounties, and the large Donations of well disposed Quality and Gentry, we and our Children have been preserved from perishing with Hunger; but especially since our Arrival in this Land of Canaan, abounding with all Things necessary and convenient for Humane Life.

"Blessed Land! Governed by the Mother of *Europe*, and the Best of Queens, in her Steadfastness and great Alacrity in Contributing largely, in all Respects, towards all her allies abroad for the speedy Reducing of the Exhorbitant Power of *France*, and our great Enemy, and likewise her Great Piety and Mild Government, and great Charity towards all Her Distressed Subjects at Home: And not Bounded here, but from afar has gathered Strangers and Despicable creatures (as a Hen her Chickens under her Wings) Scattered abroad, Destitute, Hungry, Naked, and in want of every Thing necessary for our Support.

" This great Act of Charity towards us obliges us

and our Posterity to perpetuate Her name in our
Families, and to render our Hearty Prayers to Al-
mighty God, that he will be pleased to Bless Her
Sacred Majesty with Long Life, and a Prosperous
Reign, and this Nation with a Happy Peace and
Plenty ; and for the better obtaining of which may
be given Her Repeated Victories over Her Enemies,
which are the Redundant Rewards and Blessings of
God upon Her in this Life, and may She be blest
with an Immortal Crown that never fades.

" We humbly intreat all Tradesmen not to Repine
at the good Disposition of Her Sacred Majesty, and
of the Quality and Gentry ; but with great Compassion join with them in their Charitable Disposition
towards us, and with a cheerful Readiness Receive us
at this Juncture, which we hope will be a means to
redouble the Blessings of God upon this Nation.

" We Intreat you to lay aside all Reflections and
Imprecations, and Ill Language against us, for that
is contradictory to a Christian Spirit, and we do assure you it shall be our Endeavours to act with great
Humility and Gratitude, and to render our Prayers
for you, which is all the Returns that can be made
by your[36a]

DISTRESSED BRETHREN,
The Palatines.

The English people manifested much interest in
the religious well being of these sojourners. This
arose from diverse reasons, however. It was feared

[36a] State of the Palatines, p. 6.

Umſtändige Geographiſche

Beſchreibung

Der zu allerletzt erfundenen
Provintz

PENSYLVA-
NIÆ,

In denen End-Gräntzen
AMERICÆ
In der Weſt ⚹ Welt gelegen,
Durch
FRANCISCUM DANIELEM
PASTORIUM,
J. V. Lic: und Friedens-Richtern
daſelbſten.

Worbey angehencket ſind einige no-
table Begebenheiten/ und Bericht-
Schreiben an deſſen Herrn
Vattern
MELCHIOREM ADAMUM
PASTORIUM,
Und andere gute Freunde.

Franckfurt und Leipzig/
Zufinden bey Andreas Otto. 1704.

PASTORIUS' GEOGRAPHICAL DESCRIPTION OF PENNSYLVANIA.

by some that if they remained permanently, they might join the ranks of the Dissenters; others interested themselves in their behalf because they wished to swell the ranks of the Established Church. A pamphlet was prepared in German and English for the use of the Palatines. It contained an address admonishing them to obey their Lord and Master's commands and follow in the footsteps of his disciples, and to shun the works of the devil. It also included the Sermon on the Mount and several chapters of the gospel of St. Matthew. Several pages were composed especially for their benefit; first a general thanksgiving, a prayer for the Queen, one for times of great tribulation and one for morning and night, and for God's grace and blessing.

Some of the Catholics who were of Protestant descent changed their religion with alacrity. Those who were Lutherans communed in both the German and English churches. The proprietors of the Carolinas having manifested a disposition to take married men only to their colonies, this led to numerous marriages among such as came over unmarried.

But all the while that these temporary arrangements for the care of these people were going on, the Government was not unmindful of the fact that sooner or later some permanent disposition of them must be made. In all, nearly 14,000 had come and with the exception of a few who had secured employment and were self sustaining, they were supported at the public charge. A contract was made with a

merchant in the West Indies to send five hundred
families to Barbadoes. I have not been able to find
any evidence that this contract was carried out.
Most probably it was not.

A plan to locate a large number in Ireland was
brought forward and consummated, but I have deemed
this Irish colony, in view of its numbers and character, deserving of a special chapter which will
follow.

The plan to locate them throughout the different
counties of the kingdom was not given up. Lord
Sunderland, who was the Secretary of State, wrote,
among other letters, one to the Mayor of Canterbury,
asking him to receive and permanently locate some
of them. The letter was referred to the town
Magistrates, who declined to take them upon the
ground that their own poor were a heavy burden.

But the bounty of £5 per head which, as has already been mentioned, was offered to all parishes
who would accept and settle Palatines, met with ac-
ceptance in some localities. Under its provisions,
Germans in limited numbers found their way into
all parts of England. As the bounty, rather than
the welfare of the immigrant was the main object in
view by the communities that accepted these conditions, little attention was given to them thereafter,
and they were left to take care of themselves in the
best way they could. The result was that many became dissatisfied with their lot after a while. They
found no companionship among the English, who,
as a rule, disliked as well as despised them, and, long-

ing for the association of their countrymen, many of them again found their way back to London and the various camps in the vicinity. There were some, however, who, located at great distances from the great metropolis, were from that cause, poverty and other reasons compelled to remain where they had been sent. From the large number that remains unaccounted for, after summing up those who were sent out of the country, the conclusion seems irresistible that some thousands remained for a term of years, or permanently, scattered throughout the United Kingdoms, and the city of London no doubt retained her full share.

Captain Elkin of the English navy came forward with the proposition that 600 of them should be settled on the Scilly Islands, a small group off the southwest coast of England. Lord Sunderland thought well of the project, and on September 21, and October 2, 1709, two transports were sent down the Thames with 600 men on board, well provisioned and otherwise well provided for. For some unexplained reason, these men were never sent to their destination, but after remaining on ship board three entire months, they were again set on shore on December 30, of the same year, and found their way back to Blackheath. The cost of this miserable failure was £821.18.5 for ship hire, and £665.0.6½ more for victualling the same; a total of £1486.18.-11½.

Such of them as were Catholics, and refused to become Protestants, were returned to Holland at

Queen Anne's cost, and furnished with the needed supplies to reach their own countries.

Seeing no prospects of a speedy release from their wretched condition, one hundred and fifty of the able-bodied young men enlisted in the army and were sent to serve in Lord Gallaway's regiment then on duty in Portugal. According to Luttrell's diary some also enlisted in Lord Haye's regiment. Some enlisted as sailors in the navy and were sent into foreign parts.[37] Death, too, came along and committed havoc in their ranks. More than a thousand died in the encampment at Blackheath, happy in their release from want and misery. They were reluctant to be scattered all over the British dominions. Their hope had been to be settled together in the colonies of the New World, and to this desire they remained constant throughout all their terrible experiences.

In April, 1709, the proprietors of Carolina had sold to two persons, Lewis Michell and Christopher De Graffenreid, ten thousand acres of land, in one body between the Neuse and Cape Fear rivers. Michell had previously been in the employ of the Canton of Bern, Switzerland, to look for lands in Pennsylvania, Virginia or the Carolinas, whereon a Swiss colony might be settled by that Canton, but the latter having given up the project, Michell and his partner conceived the idea of bringing over colo-

---

[37] "Etliche Sind mit der Ost Indischen Flatte in Ost Indien gangen, und daselbs zerstrenet." Das verlangte, nicht erlangte Canaan, p. 8.

Außführlich
und
Umständlicher Bericht ·
Von der berühmten Landschafft

CAROLINA,

In dem
Engelländischen America
gelegen.

An Tag gegeben
Von

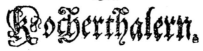

Kocherthalern.

Zweyter Druck.

Franckfurt am Mayn/
Zu finden bey Georg Heinrich Oehrling/
Anno 1709.

PAMPHLET CIRCULATED BY KOCHERTHAL, ADVISING EMIGRANTS
TO GO TO THE CAROLINAS.

nists themselves.[38] The Palatines became the object
of their speculative enterprise, and they covenanted
with the English Commissioners, that the latter
should send over about one hundred families, in all
about 650 persons, and locate them on these lands.
The Commissioners allowed five pounds per head for
the transporting of these settlers, supplied them with
provisions for twelve months, and in addition gave
them twenty shillings each out of the funds which
had been raised by popular subscription. The colonists reached the confluence of the Neuse and Trent
rivers in December, 1709, and were housed in temporary shelters. In accordance with instructions from
the home government, Governor Tryon allotted 100
acres to each man, woman and child.

A large number, perhaps as many as two or three
thousand, were returned to the places from which
they had originally come. Luttrell mentions that in
May, 1710, Minister Dayrolle gave five florins each
to 800 Palatines who were returned to their homes.
Some of these, as we have already seen, were Catholics, but many Protestants were also sent along, it
being found impossible to dispose of them otherwise.

The last large body to be sent away was the well-
known colony that went to the State of New York
under the plan submitted by Col. Hunter, then recently appointed Governor of that province, to the
Board of Trade. It is not necessary that I should
go into the details of this scheme, as they are

[38] Williamson's North Carolina.

familiar to all, and will be fully dealt with in a future paper of this series. It is enough to say that three thousand two hundred were crowded into ten small ships and set sail in March, 1710. They arrived at intervals between June 14 and July 24. Four hundred and seventy perished on the voyage. Not all, however, left England. Some had found permanent employment and a few had entered into business. Some worked in her Majesty's gardens and others on a canal at Windsor. A little hamlet arose on the west side of London where some houses had been erected for the use of these people, and to this day they bear the name of the Palatine houses.[39]

An account written at the period, gives us an insight into their manner of living at that time:

LONDON: Printed for *J. Baker*, at the *Black-Boy.* in *Pater Noster-Row.* 1710.

THIS QUAINT WOOD CUT OF THE PERIOD SHOWS HOW THESE PEOPLE PASSED THEIR TIME WHILE CAMPED AT BLACKHEATH.

"They spend their time very religiously and industriously, having prayers morning and evening,

---

[39] H. A. Holmes.

with singing of psalms, and preaching every Sunday, where both old and young appear very serious and devout. Some employ themselves in making several toys of small value, which they sell to the multitudes that come daily to see them. They are contented with very ordinary food, their bread being brown, and their meat of the coarsest and cheapest sort, which, with a few roots and herbs, they eat with much cheerfulness and thankfulness. Great numbers of them go every Sunday to their church in the Savoy and receive the Sacrament of their own ministers. Many of the younger are married every week; the women wear rosemary and the men laurel in their hair at the time of their marriage, adultery and fornication being much abhorred by them. When any are buried, all the attendants go singing after the corpse, and when they come to the grave the coffin is opened for all to see the body. After it is

PALATINES WORSHIPPING IN ST. MARY'S, OF SAVOY.

laid in the ground they all sigh again for some time and then depart. They carry grown people upon a bier and children upon their heads. On the whole they appear to be an innocent, laborious, peaceable, healthy and ingenious people, and may be rather reckoned a blessing than a burden to any nation where they shall be settled."

To give some idea of the class of persons who composed this great body of immigrants, the following list is submitted. I have found a number of such lists,[40] but the one I quote is the fullest of them all and no doubt as reliable as any. This authority says that "from the middle of April, 1709, till the middle of July, the arrivals in London were 11,294 German Protestants, males and females. Of the males there were : husbandmen and vine dressers, 1838 ; bakers, 78 ; masons, 477 ; carpenters, 124 ; shoemakers, 68 ; tailors, 99 : butchers, 29 ; millers, 45 ; tanners, 14 ; stocking weavers, 7 ; saddlers, 13 ; glass blowers, 2 ; hatters, 3 ; lime burners, 8 ; schoolmasters, 18 ; engravers, 2 ; brickmakers, 3 ; silversmiths, 2 ; smiths, 35 ; herdsmen, 3 ; blacksmiths, 48 ; potters, 3 ; turners, 6 ; barbers, 1 ; surgeons, 2. Of these 11,294 there were 2556 who had families."[41]

---

[40] State of the Palatines.
Rupp's note in Rush's Essay on the manners and customs of the Germans of Pennsylvania.

[41] As a matter of interest a second enumeration is given from Frank's *"Frankfurter Mesz-Kalender von Ostern bis Herbst,"* 1709, which says that by the middle of July 6520 Germans had arrived in London. Of these 1278 were men with families, 1238 married women, 89 widows, 384 young men, 106 young women, 379 boys over 14 years old, 374 girls over 14 years old, 1363 boys under 14 and 1309 girls under 14 years. Among these people were 1083 husbandmen and vine dressers, 90

Kurtze
Beschreibung
Des H. N. Reichs Stadt
Windsheim/

Sámt

Dero vielfältigen Unglücks-Fällen/
und wahrhafftigen Ursachen ihrer so grossen Decadenz und Erbarmungs-würdigen Zustandes/

Aus

Alten/ glaubwürdigen Documentis und Briefflichen Urkunden (der itzo-lebenden lieben Burgerschafft/ und Dero Nachkommen/ zu guter Nachricht) also zusammen getragen/ und in den Druck gegeben

durch

Melchiorem Adamum Paftorium,
áltern Burgemeiftern und Ober-Richtern in befagter Stadt.

Gedruckt zu Nürnberg
bey Christian Sigmund Froberg.
Im Jahr Christi 1692.

Fortunately for us, who are at this distant day attempting to unravel the twisted threads which encumber the story of these poor Palatines, there lived in London at that time a man of education, leisure, and thoroughly acquainted with public affairs. His name was Narcissus Luttrell. One of his pleasures was to keep a diary. This diary is very full and minute, but unlike the better known diarist who preceded him, the inimitable Pepys, he devoted his pages more to public affairs and less to himself. From day to day, for a period of 36 years, he recorded the World's news as it reached London. Every thing was set down as it came. He appears to have been without bias or prejudices and as the result, his diary appears to be a complete picture of the times as they passed before him. It contains numerous allusions to this Palatine immigration, and as it is little known, I will here quote such remarks as I have found in it bearing on this question.

"1709 Thursday, May 12. From Cologne that three great vessels more were arrived there with Protestants from the Palatines for England, and thence to Pennsylvania; so that above 1000 families have already quitted that country.

"Saturday, 14 May. A great many poor German and French Protestants have taken the oaths this

---

carpenters, 34 bakers, 48 masons, 20 joiners, 40 shoemakers, 58 tailors, 15 butchers, 27 millers, 7 tanners, 4 stocking weavers, 6 barbers, 3 locksmiths, 13 smiths, 46 linen and cloth weavers, 48 coopers, 13 wheelwrights, 5 hunters, 7 saddlers, 2 glass blowers, 2 hatters, 8 lime and tile burners, 1 cook, 10 schoolmasters, 1 student, 2 engravers, 7 farmers.

week at the Queen's bench court, in order to their naturalization by the late act.

"Saturday, 28 May. Sunday last about 300 Protestants from the Palatinate received the sacrament at the Prussian church in Savoy, in order to their naturalization; 1300 more are also arrived, and a sermon will be preached before them once a week in Aldgate church.

"Tuesday, 14 June. Sunday Monsieur du Quesne, a French Protestant, presented a letter to her majestie from the King of Prussia about the Reformed churches in France, and a petition in the name of above a million of those poor people who groan under a most severe persecution; she assured him she had already given her ministers abroad instructions concerning the same, and will doe for them what else lies in her power.

"Thursday, 16 June. The justices of the Middlesex have resolved to petition her majestie for a brief to support the poor Palatines come over hither, being upward of 6000.

"Saturday, 18 June. Tis said a brief was then ordered (in council) for a collection in London and Middlesex to relieve the poor Palatines, and that the Commissioners of Trade and Plantations are to take care of them till the West India fleet goes, when they are to embark for Nevis and St. Christophers, to re-people those islands destroyed by the French.

"Tuesday, 21 June. Tents are putting up at Blackheath for the poor Palatines till they can be transported to the West Indies.

" Thursday, 7 July. Yesterday the nobility and gentry, commissioners for providing for the support of the poor Palatines lately arrived here, met the first time in the convocation house at St. Paul's, where were present the Lord Mayor and several of the aldermen.

" Tuesday, 12 July. Monsieur Ruperti is translating the liturgy of the church of England into High Dutch, which books are to be given among the poor Palatines, 2000 more of whom last Sunday arrived here from Rotterdam.

" Saturday, 16 July. The lords proprietors of Carolina have made proposals to a committee of Council, to take all the Palatines here, from 15 to 45 years old and send them to their plantation; but her majestie to be at the charge of transporting them, which will be above £10 a head.

"Saturday, 23 July. 300 more Palatines are arrived, so that the whole number here is about 8000.

"Saturday, 1 August. Several of the poor Palatines who came lately over, and were Papists, have renounced that religion, and more of them, 'tis expected, will do the like.

"Thursday, 4 August. Mr. Paul Girard at an eminent French refugee merchant in Coleman street, has upon the brief for the poor Palatines, given £423 towards their relief, and several other citizens very liberally.

"Tuesday, 9 August. The Commissioners for providing for the poor Palatines, upon inspecting the subscriptions of the nobility and gentry, find that

CONTINUATIO

Der

Beschreibung der Landschafft

PENSYLVANIÆ

An denen End-Gräntzen

AMERICÆ.

Uber vorige des Herrn Pastorii Relationes.

In sich haltend:

Die Situation, und Fruchtbarkeit des Erdbodens. Die Schiffreiche und andere Flüsse. Die Anzahl derer bißhero gebauten Städte. Die seltsame Creaturen an Thieren / Vögeln und Fischen. Die Mineralien und Edelgesteine Deren eingebohrnen wilden Völcker Sprachen / Religion und Gebräuche. Und die ersten Christlichen Pflantzer und Anbauer dieses Landes.

Beschrieben von

GABRIEL THOMAS

15. Jährigen Inwohner dieses Landes.

Welchem Tractätlein noch beygefüget sind:

Des Hn. DANIEL FALCKNERS

Burgers und Pilgrims in Pensylvania 193. Beantwortungen uff vorgelegte Fragen von guten Freunden.

Franckfurt und Leipzig /
Zu finden bey Andreas Otto / Buchhändlern.

about £15,000 is already given for their support. Abundance of them are gone hence in wagons for Chester to embark for Ireland, and the rest designed for that Kingdom will speedily follow.

" Thursday, 15 September. The Popish Palatines who came hither, are ordered to go home, having passports for the same.

. "Thursday, 29 September. Yesterday 18 Palatines listed themselves in the Lord Haye's regiment.

"Thursday, 6 Oct. The commissioners for settling the poor Palatines have resolved to send forthwith 600 of them to Carolina, and 1500 of them to New York ; and 'tis said, the merchants of Bediford and Barnstable, concerned in the Newfoundland fishery, intend to employ 500 more in their service.

" Thursday, 29 Dec. Colonel Hunter (the new Governor of New York,) designs next week to embark for his government of New York ; and most of the Palatines remaining here goe with him to people that colony.

"1710. Thursday, 25 May. Mr. Ayrolles, the British Secretary at the Hague, is gone for Rotterdam to distribute her majesties charity to 800 poor Palatines returning home, being 5 florins to each person.

. "Thursday, 27 July. The first ticket of the State lottery drawn yesterday entitled the fortunate holder to £50 per annum, and fell upon Mr. Walter Cocks of Camberwell, who so generously supported the Palatines last year, and has this year the best crop of corn for quantity in all the county of Surrey."

THE GERMAN COLONY IN IRELAND.[42]

ITS FOUNDING AND ITS VICISSITUDES—IT INTRODUCED THE
LINEN INDUSTRY INTO THAT COUNTRY—WHAT TRAVELLERS
HAVE HAD TO SAY OF ITS PEOPLE AND THEIR CONDITION.

SEAL OF THE CITY OF LIMERICK.

I RETURN now to those Germans who were not sent to America, who were not returned to their own country, and who did not remain in England, the 3800 souls that were colonized in Ireland. Beyond the few brief allusions to their transportation to that country found in modern writers, comparatively little concerning them is known to the general reader. I shall, therefore, proceed to give with some detail, the information that has rewarded my research concerning them.

As we have already seen, the attempt to settle these people permanently in England met with no favor and had to be abandoned. The plan to send some to Ireland and locate them permanently there, apparently met with no opposition. In fact, the proposition to make this disposal of them originated in Ireland itself. The Committee appointed to inquire into the coming of the Palatines into Great Britain, and upon what encouragement, in their report to the House of Commons on April 14, 1711, said that the plan for locating some of them in Ireland, originated in that country itself. Mr. J. Marshall, Deputy Master of the Rolls of Tipperary, offered to assume the care of 1000, and build houses for them. At the request of the Lord Lieutenant and Council of Ireland, he addressed the Queen on the subject, asking that as many Palatines should be sent there as her Majesty should think proper. In

---

[42] The following order was issued from White Hall, July 27, 1709 : "The Right Honorable the Lord Lieutenant and Council of Ireland, having in an Humble Address to her Majesty, Requested, that as many of the poor Palatines as her Majesty shall see fit, may be settled in that Kingdom, and given Assurances that they shall be very Kindly received, and advantageously settled there ; and the address having been laid before the Right Honorable, the Lords and others, her Majesty's Commissioners, for receiving and disposing of the money to be collected for the subsistence and settlement of the said Palatines The said Commissioners have resolved that Five Hundred Families of the said Palatines be forthwith sent into that Kingdom, and refer it to their Committee to settle the manner and time of sending them thither.''

August, 1709, 500 families, numbering in all 3000 persons, were sent to that country, The cost of sending them there as disclosed in the Parliamentary report, was £3498.16.6. To complete their settlement in Ireland a warrant was drawn and signed by Queen Anne, for the sum of £15,000, to be paid out of her Majesty's revenues in that country, and to be repaid in three years, at the rate of £5000 every year.

The report to the Commons informs us that in Feb. 1710, 800 more Palatines were sent from London by way of Chester or Liverpool, to Ireland, upon representations from the Lord Lieutenant, the crown again bearing the charges, and £9000 were allotted for their better settlement, this sum, like the former one, being also made a charge on the Irish revenues. Presently, however, it was found that some of these families were returning to England again, and that still others were preparing to follow them. Whereupon the Commissioners sent an agent, one John Crockett, to prevent, if possible, any further migrations. Upon arriving in Ireland, he found 20 families ready to go on board a vessel to return to England, they having a pass for 25 families. This pass was signed by the Lord Lieutenant's Steward, John Smalles. Crockett however stopped them and took away their pass. An appeal was taken to the highest legal tribunal and he was informed by Lord Chief Justice Broderick, that being a free people, they could not be legally prevented from going where they would. That decision seems to have effectually disposed of Agent Crockett and his mission. Within

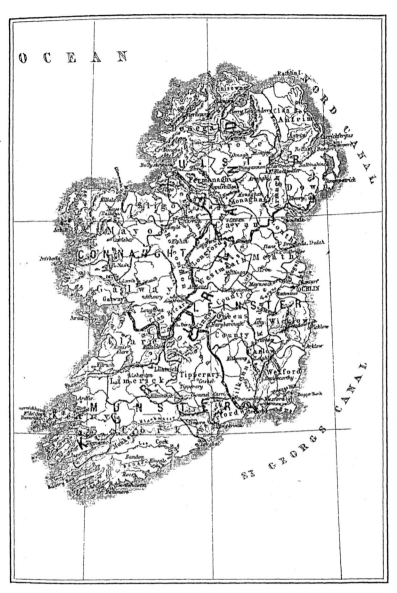

Map of Ireland at the time of the German Exodus.

a brief period thereafter, 232 more families returned to Southwark.

The reasons these Palatines gave for leaving Ireland, was the rough usage received from the Commissary in whose charge they were, a man named Huick, from a Mr. Street, and others, who did not pay them their subsistance, they having received but one week's allowance. They paid their own passage to England, although they were told they should have ten shillings per head for leaving Ireland. From all this we think we have ample reasons to infer that this German colony partook somewhat of the nature of a speculation in which the public officials took a leading part. Why was the Lord Lieutenant of Ireland so anxious to get them into that country, and why was he so busily employed in sending them away again, after the large allowances for their maintenance had been received? Even the pittance of ten shillings, which appears to have been the bribe offered them to go back again, it seems was not paid. Apparently, there was an undercurrent of fraud throughout on the part of the minor and higher officials.

The motives for sending these Palatines to Ireland was by no means an unselfish one, even on the part of the Government itself, or intended only to better their condition. Being Protestants the House of Commons was of the opinion that so large a body of that creed would not only tranquilize, but contribute to the stability and security of the Kingdom which has not yet recovered from the shock of the battle of the Boyne, fought only twenty years before. To a certain extent this last aim was defeated because their treatment and deception by the government agents drove some of them away before they were quietly settled down.

They were located on some unimproved lands at

Rathkeale, near Limerick, in the County of Munster. Kapp says that among the first 500 families sent to Ireland were all the linen weavers, and this is also spoken of by other writers.[43] Whether the linen industry was prominent in Ireland prior to this invasion of the Palatines I have not been able to ascertain, but it is a matter of history that in the year 1711, two years after this colony was founded, a government board of manufacturers was established in Ireland, which, by means of a system of bounties and in other ways did its utmost to encourage the linen trade.[44] These facts

ARMS OF THE BISHOP OF LIMERICK.

---

[43] Friedrich Kapp. Geschichtsblätter, p. 23.

[44] Anton Eickhoff: In der neuen Heimath ; Geschichtliche Mittheilungen uber die deutchen einwanderer in aller Theilen der Uuion, has copied Kapp verbatim. Kapp's words are: "Zuerst 500 Familien, darunter alle Leinweber, etc."

seem to warrant the belief, that if these German colonists did not in fact, first establish the linen trade in that country, they at all events gave it such an impulse with their skill as to have for nearly two hundred years made it the most important textile industry in Ireland.[45] Such it is to-day.

In 1715, Parliament passed a special act authorizing the naturalization of those who were still there, 213 families in all. Of those who went away, about 75 families returned to London, from whence they were sent to this country. For a number of years afterward, numbers of them kept coming to Pennsylvania. The expense of sending them to Ireland and their settlement there, cost the English government £24,000.

From the fact that for a good many years little was heard of this colony, we may infer that German thrift and industry were making their mark there, as they have done the whole world over; that they pursued the even tenor of their way, and gave little care to what was going on around them.

Under the distinctive " name of Palatines, they left the impress of their character in social and economical traits on the whole district, extending from Castle Mattrass eastward to Adare."[46]

John Wesley, the eminent evangelist, and founder of Methodism, during a trip to Ireland, in 1758, paid a visit to this Palatine colony. In his Journal he

---

[45] Chamber's Encyclopaedia, vol. vi.
[46] Holmes.

Teusday evening

The enclosed petitions veare given me as I came from S.t James, one I beleve is from y.e man you gave me an account of yesterday, y.e other haveing a wife & six children makes me think it a case of Compassion, how-ever I desire you now informe your self about it as soon as you can possible, & if you find it soe, take care his life may be saved, I am

Your very affectionate freind   ANNE R.

It affords me much pleasure to be able to present the above brief but most interesting autograph letter of Queen Anne. There is no address and no evidence to show to whom it was written. The familiar tone seems to indicate that the person was one of her political household. Possibly it may have been to one of the clergymen who played so prominent a part in this drama of exile although this is not likely. Be this as

tells what he saw while there. He says: "I rode over to Court Mattrass, a colony of Germans, whose parents came out of the Palatinate fifty years ago. Twenty families settled here; twenty more at Killikeen, a mile off; fifty at Balligarene, about two miles eastward, and twenty at Pallas, four miles further. Each family had a few acres of ground, on which they built as many little houses. They are since considerably increased in number of families. Having no minister, they were becoming eminent for drunkenness, cursing, swearing, and an utter neglect of religion. But they are washed since they heard the truth which is able to save their souls. An oath is now rarely heard among them, or a drunkard seen in their borders. Court Mattrass is built in the form of a square, in the middle of which they have placed a pretty large preaching house."[47] In 1760, some of the descendants of these Irish Palatines left Limerick for the United States, and were among the pioneers of American Methodism. John Wesley had made a good many converts among these people while he was with them, the principal having been Philip Embury, (Amberg) and his son Samuel, the latter having come to New York in 1760.[48]

---

it may, however, we have in this most kind and womanly note, confirming evidence of the unselfish interest this noble Queen felt in these people.

The original of this letter is in the incomparable collection of Ferdinand J. Dreer, Esq., of Philadelphia. This fac-simile is here, by permission, for the first time, given to the public.

[47] See Wesley's Journal.

[48] Rupp's unpublished MSS. See Seidensticker's German Day, p. 17.

Eight acres of land, according to one account, were set aside for each one of these Germans at five shillings per acre, and the Government pledged itself to pay the ground taxes for them, for a period of twenty years.

An English "Blue Book" states that "they were a frugal and industrious people. Their number, however, has been greatly diminished through later emigrations to America, and at the present day (period unknown) there are proportionately but few descendants of these in Ireland."

In 1780, Farrar, the historian of Limerick, wrote of them as follows: "The Palatines still retain their language, but it is on the point of declining. They elect a Burgomaster, to whom they appeal in all cases of dispute. They are industrious and have leases from the landlords at reasonable rents. They are better fed and clothed than the Irish farmers. Their husbandry and harvests are better than those of their Irish neighbors. By degrees they abandoned their 'Saur Kraut' and lived on potatoes, milk, butter, oat and wheat bread, and poultry. They sleep between two beds (feather beds), huge flitches of bacon hang from the rafters, and massive chests hold the household linen : their superstitions savor of the banks of the Rhine : in their dealings they are upright and honorable."

In 1840, Mr. and Mrs. S. C. Hall, the well known authors, also visited and wrote about this old German colony. They said : "They differ from other people of the country. The elder people still retain their language, customs and religion, but the younger ones mingle with the Irish people and intermarry with them."

In May of the same year, Dr. Michell writes: "The majority of them have decidedly foreign features, and are of sturdy build. Their countenance is of a dark hue, their hair dark and their eyes brown. A comparison of the inhabitants of the Bavarian Palatinate shows them to be light of complexion and blue eyed. This argues that the Irish Palatines have intermarried with the Irish natives. The old comfortable homes of these people are falling into decay, and newer dwellings have arisen nearby, some of them two stories high, with slate roofs. Almost all of them have gardens, and some orchards attached. Economy and industry prevail among them. The names of the Palatines in Ireland differ but little from those of people with the same origin. Some of their names are Baker, Miller, Lodwig, Modlar, Pyfer, Reynard, Shire, and Stark, which were originally Becker, Müller, Ludwig. Pfeiffer, Reinhardt and Shier.[50]

An intelligent traveller who made a tour of Ireland in 1840, and wrote a book about the country, throws out a most interesting suggestion in what he has to say of these people. This is what he writes: "It was also with much regret that I forebore from visiting a German colony that settled in the county of Limerick about the beginning of the last century.

---

[50] See article in the Philadelphia Record, a year or two ago.

The settlers were from the Palatinate, and their descendants are still called Palatinates, though they have lost the language of their fathers. They have not, however, lost the German character for good order and honorable dealing, and are looked upon as the best farmers in the country. 'They are a most respectable people,' said an Irish lady to me, 'and much wealthier and far better off than any of their Irish neighbors.'

"It is a constant subject of discussion in Ireland, between the Irish patriots and the adherents of the English, that is between the Celtomanes and the Anglomanes, whether the misery and poverty of Ireland ought to be attributed to the tyranny and bad government of the English, or whether the indolence and want of energy of the Irish themselves be not in a great measure to blame. Now the prosperity of this German colony, though subject to the same laws and influences as the native Irish, would seem not to decide the question in favor of the friends of the Celts. Upon the whole, however, there are not many Germans in Ireland, not even in Dublin. They were probably never more numerous there than during the rebellion in 1798, when several regiments of Hanoverians were employed in the country, and their presence in such form may not have left a very favorable impression respecting them on the public mind."[51]

Several authorities confirm the fact that as late as

[51] Ireland. By J. G. Kohl, 1844.

1855, the descendants of these German-Irish colonists were still living in the county of Limerick and that to some extent they still retained many of their original characteristics along with their industry and thrift, and were scrupulously honorable in all their dealings. They were still, for the most part, prosperous farmers and weavers, and stood well in the community.[52]

We are, therefore, warranted in believing that on the whole, this Irish colony is to be regarded as having emerged from its troubles and trials as well, if not better, than any of the unwelcome visitors that poured into London in the spring and summer of 1709. It is true, some were dissatisfied and left, as has already been shown. Those who remained escaped the pest ships, and the tyranny that awaited them in the State of New York and elsewhere. Their greatest trials had come to an end, and thence forward neither religious nor political troubles molested them, while want and starvation existed only as unhappy memories.

---

[52] Meth. Quar. Rev. Oct. 1855.
See also Fliegende Blætter 11.36.

CONCLUSION.

ARMS OF WURTEMBERG.

IT will be seen from the foregoing, that the large number which is said to have come to London, is not fully accounted for in the enumeration of those who were sent to Ireland, to the New World or returned to their own country again. Kapp, a reliable guide in general, fixes the total number of emigrants at between 13,000 and 14,000 souls. But he fails to dispose of that number when he comes to sum up. Löher goes far beyond him and says ship load after ship load reached London, until their number in the Blackheath camp reached 32,468. It would be interesting to know where he got his extravagant figures. There is no warrant for them in any published documents that I have seen, nor in the unpublished archives of England and Holland so far as they have been examined.

In this statement he is, however, followed by several later writers, who bring forward no evidence nor authority for their estimates. They seem to have followed Löher blindly. The statement, therefore, made by the latest author who has dealt with this phase of the question, that " During the two years 1708 and 1709, over thirty thousand of them crossed over to England,[53] is wholly unsustained by the authorities, figures and facts to which I have had access.

Careful accounts of all the expenditures incurred by the British Government are to be found in the Journals of Parliament, and the records of the Board of Trade, and the sum total has been figured out. They include the costs incurred by the several schemes which have here been enumerated and nothing more. Had the Palatines been 32,000 instead of 14,000 or less, the cost must also have been doubled. As here given, the following numbers are accounted for :

Sent to Ireland,	3,800
Colonized in North Carolina,	650
Sent to New York,	3,200
Returned to Germany, (perhaps)	2,000
Died in England,	1,500
Enlisted, (perhaps)	350
Total	11,500

This enumeration leaves about two thousand un-accounted for. It is very probable that not all were sent out of the country, because some had found acceptable employment, while many left at inter-vals during the next few years. That some re-mained in London years after the great body of them had been disposed of is absolutely proven by a writer under the date of June, 1712, who says: "On my return (from Kensington and Hyde Park), I saw a number of the Palatines, the most poor, ragged creatures that I ever saw, and great objects of charity, if real exiles for religion.[54]

---

[53] Sydney George Fisher : The Making of Pennsylvania.
[54] Ralph Thoresly Diary, 1674-1724. 2 vols. 8 vo. London, 1830.

ARMS OF HANOVER.

COST OF MAINTAINING THESE GERMANS.

IT MEANT MORE THAN HALF A MILLION DOLLARS TO THE
ENGLISH GOVERNMENT—BUT IT WAS MONEY WELL SPENT.

ARMS OF FRANKFURT.

ALL Germans, and more especially we Americans of German descent, owe a heavy debt of gratitude to Great Britain, the Government as well as her individual citizens, for what they did for those forlorn and distressed Palatines. While there can be no manner of doubt that the Government covertly, if not openly, connived at this immigration, there is also every reason to believe that it finally assumed far greater proportions than were looked for in the beginning; and, therefore, proved far more costly than was at first anticipated.

From first to last, and during every stage of its

progress, this remarkable episode proved a very
costly affair to the English government. The
records are still accessible, and from them the following statement is prepared :

To Kocherthal and his followers, £346.00; for the
maintenance of these people at Rotterdam, and their
transportation to England, £6199.3.2; collected by
public subscription in London, and throughout the
country, £19,838.11.1; cost of the Scilly Islands
fiasco, £1487.18.11½ ; sending the colony to Ireland
and expenses incurred thereby, £24,000; the cost of
sending the remaining large body to New York,
£38,000; the Secretary of the Navy also expended
£8,000 in various ways; there were besides many
other charges for smaller amounts, which ran the
figures up to a total of £135,775.18. There is some
doubt whether the entire sum voted for the settlement of the Irish colony was paid out, or the total
allotted for the care of those sent to New York, but
this is not material. Here we have more than a half
a million dollars paid out, at a period when England
was not so rich as she is now, and at a time, too, when
she was engaged in costly foreign wars, and when
money was worth much more than it is to-day.
While it is perhaps true that mercenary motives may
have had much to do with her early action, it is also
undoubtedly true that her Government was far-
sighted enough to understand, that the accession of
so many of the best citizens of one of the richest
provinces in the Old World, must have its due effect
upon the welfare and prosperity of the colonies she

Curieuſe Nachricht
Von
PENSYLVANIA
in
Norden = America
Welche /
Auf Begehren guter Freunde/
Über vorgelegte 103. Fragen / bey ſeiner Abreiß auß Teutſchland nach obigem Lande Anno 1700.
ertheilet/ und nun Anno 1702 in den Druck
gegeben worden.
Von
Daniel Falcknern/ Profeſſore,
Burgern und Pilgrim allda.

Franckfurt und Leipzig /
Zu finden bey Andreas Otto/Buchhändlern.
Im Jahr Chriſti 1702.

had planted beyond the Atlantic. Nor was she mistaken in this. That German immigration has continued until this very hour, and the American continent from ocean to ocean bears the impress of German thrift, culture, progress and prosperity.

It is a wonderful story I have tried to tell. All history may be challenged to match it. There was unyielding resolution, determined perseverance, courage under the most adverse circumstances, a purpose that knew no shadow of turning, and a faith and a heroism that win our admiration and command our respect through all the years that have come and gone. These are the qualities that shine through all the trials and misadventures that befell these sturdy sons of the Fatherland.

The silver-tipped tongue of the orator, the pencil of the artist and the lyre of the poet cannot adequately tell the tale, and while the divine hand of Clio shall guide the eloquent pen of history, she will find no theme more worthy of her mission than this story of our ancestors, staking their all upon an uncertain venture into the New World. Bearing aloft that grand motto of their race, *Ohne Hast, ohne Rast,* they pressed onward toward the goal of their hopes with the same energy, determination and unflinching courage with which their ancestors seventeen centuries before had defied the power of Rome, and hurled back the legions of Cæsar.

APPENDIX.

A STREET CANAL IN ROTTERDAM.

APPENDICES.

PREFATORY NOTE.

HERE are no surer nor safer guides for the chronicler of historical events, than the narratives to be found in contemporary records, especially when such records emanate from impartial sources and were never intended for publication. The carefully recorded minutes of a municipality or a Board of Administration endowed with executive functions, not only furnish a basis whereon the narrator may safely build, but they are at the same time certain to supply material not to be found elsewhere, thus becoming doubly valuable.

The unpublished records of the city of Rotterdam, and the Journal of the Proceedings of the English Commissioners for Promoting the Trade of the Kingdom, have been some of the sources from which part of the facts in the preceding narrative have been drawn. I have therefore thought it not without interest, if extracts from both these sources were given in this connection.

A great deal of other interesting material which could not properly be presented, either in the text or the notes, also accumulated on my hands, and I have utilized it here as throwing further light on the story of this Exodus.

APPENDIX A.

[A translation of some of the municipal records of the city of Rotterdam, and other documents, relating to the passage of the German emigrants through Holland, to England. From original copies obtained at Rotterdam and the Hague, by Julius F. Sachse, Esq., and now in the possession of the Historical Society of Pennsylvania. F. R. D.]

Extract from the Resolutions and Proceedings of the Burgomasters of Rotterdam :

ARMS OF ROTTERDAM.

PRIL 22, 1709, all of the Lords Burgomasters being present, it was resolved to pay over to Engel Kon and Samuel de Back, four hundred and fifty guilders, to be distributed among destitute families of the Lower Palatinate, for their subsistence on their journey, via England, to Pennsylvania, and a warrant shall be drawn.

April 29, 1709, all the Lords Burgomasters being present, it was resolved to pay over to Peter Toomen, a sum of three hundred guilders, for distribution among destitute families, who arrived after those heretofore mentioned from the Lower Palatinate, for their subsistence as far as Pennsylvania, and a warrant shall be drawn.

A true copy.

UNGER,

Archivist of the City of Rotterdam.

An Extract from the Resolutions and Dispositions of Burgomasters:

Rec. 3.   Sheet 126, vol. 127.

PEOPLE COMING FROM THE PALATINATE TO GO TO ENGLAND.

August 12, 1709, all of the Lords Burgomasters being present, Mr. Joh. Steenhak excepted.

In consequence of a report of Hendrick Toren and Jan van Gent, concerning people from the Palatinate, already arrived and still to be expected, and others coming in great numbers from Germany, it was agreed to despatch eight notices, as follows :

"Burgomasters and Regents of the city of Rotterdam, hereby give notice, as a warning to the multitude of people who are coming over in great crowds from Germany, with the intention of being transported from here to England, and from there to Pennsylvania, and where they further may belong, that from exhibition of original letters and extracts and otherwise, it has appeared to Their Right Honorables, that Her Majesty of Great Britain has given orders not to send over any more of the said people to Her Majesty's charge, so long as those who are now in England have not been disposed of further. Their High Honorables give notice that Hendrick Toom and Jan van Gent, out of Christian charity and compassion, have taken pains, by order of her said Majesty, to provide for transportation and other necessities : that they are men of honor and perfect trustworthiness, and especially that in this case they have been requested and authorized, as they are again requested and authorized by these presents, to give and cause to be given notice hereof in such manner as they shall judge can properly and most effectually be done, to these of the Palatinate and others, who for the said purpose might intend to come over from Germany, thus preventing the said people from making a fruitless voyage to Holland. In witness whereof we have had some copies of these presents made and affixed thereto the seal of this city, and the signature of our Clerk, this 12 of August, 1709.

———

NOTE : August 24th, 1709. Present, the Lords Mar. Grolmna and Ads. Boosemele to the said Toom and Van Gent, who for eight days have been about with two yachts, one on the river Waal and the other on the river Maas, the sum of three hundred and fifty guilders is appropriated for their expenses, by ordinance of Burgomasters, as through the precaution taken by them, probably a thousand people who were on the road have gone back, so that according to all appearances those poor people shall be gotten rid of. And further the said Toom and Van Gent have been requested to take pains to travel up stream themselves in order to intercept those coming off with promise of indemnification of expenses in this case to be disbursed.

Extract from a letter sent to the Burgomasters of Rotterdam, by the Burgomasters and Regents of the city of Brielle. Pages 1707-1713, vol. 23.

RIGHT HONORABLE LORDS.

Among the people from the Palatinate, as well as from Hesse and other German quarters who have come down and are here lying in vessels at the pier, there are a great number who have not sufficient vituals to pursue their journey and many of whom are coming daily asking about their support, which for our small city is impossible, the poor pence being exhausted by the long continued support of soldiers' wives and children, whose husbands and fathers are in Spain ; wherefore we pray your right Honorables to have the goodness to relieve the

poverty of these indigent and suffering people, and to assist
them, as we are unable to do so alone, and otherwise, in case of
continuation, we would be obliged to send them back in boats to
Rotterdam.   We shall therefore hope that out of consideration
your Right Honorables will not let them die of hunger and
thirst, but lend a helping hand that these poor people may
accomplish their intended journey.

Wherewith Right Honorable Lords we commend your
Right Honorables to God's protection and remain

> Your Right Honorables good friends
> Burgomaster and Regents
> of the city of Brielle.
> By order of the same.
>   P. D. JAGEN.

BRIELLE, Aug. 24, 1709.

An extract from letter book No. 10 of the Burgomasters of Rotterdam :

TO THE VERY HONORABLE LORDS, BURGOMASTERS AND RE-
GENTS OF THE CITY OF BRIELLE.

We can easily understand that your very Honorable City
has to have much annoyance from people coming from Germany,
but your very Honorables can also perceive therefrom how
much greater the annoyance in this matter has been and still is
for our city (even in proportion to the difference in population
of both cities) for here has been and still is the first arrival, and
it is here that orders, ships, convoy, wind and what not is
waited for.   The charity of our inhabitants towards these people
is uncommon indeed, which certainly must reflect seriously on
our own poor.   Nevertheless, we have been obliged from time
to time, to assist from the city treasury, so as to prevent calamities which might arise from the utter indigency of so large a
crowd of people ; and besides many sick and feble ones are in
our city who remain to our charge.   From all of which your
Very Honorables will please pay some attention to it.   We

trust that your very Honorables shall reach the conclusion that in the whole country there is no city or place where the burden might be discharged with less reason than upon our city.

Moreover, these poor people have not the slightest relation to us whatever : wherefore we also have such complete confidence in your very Honorable's equity, that the same shall desist from the measures mentioned in their letter of the 24th, namely, the request of our assistance and much more, the sending of these poor people to our city. From the beginning we have applied all possible means on the one hand to transport those who had already arrived, in the quickest way possible, to England, and on the other hand to direct new arrivals as much as possible, both of which precautions have not only cost us much trouble but also much money, and we have especially at our expense, sent two merchants in two yachts up the rivers Waal and Teck which has had such effect that at least a thousand people have been diverted and that by their example others will likely change their mind. Without these precautions the hardships to your Honorable city would certainly have been much greater. If your Honorables wish to come and counsel with us about these measures, or about seeking help from the Government, we on our side will be prepared therefor, and we also will instruct on this subject, the Lords Deputies of this city to the assembly of their High Mightinesses. Therewith, very Honorable Lords, we recommend you to God's merciful protection.

Written at Rotterdam, this 26th of August, 1709. Your very Honorables' good friends, the

BURGOMASTERS AND REGENTS
of the city of Rotterdam.

Extract from the record of resolutions of the States General of the United Netherlands, 1709, vol. 2, fol. 348.

MONDAY, Sept. 16, 1709.
President, Lord Hocut. Present, Lord Van Welderen,

Van Oldersom, Pols, Van Essen, Niu Winckel, Menthen Hain, and the Extraordinary Deputy from the Province of Gelderland Hegcoop, Groenewegen, Van Waters, Van Dorp, Velders, Woorthey, Degm, Meerens, Grand Pensionary Heinsius, Harinxmotoe, Staten and Du Four.

The resolutions taken on the day before yesterday were called up. To the assembly was read a memorandum from Secretary Dayrolles, requesting that it may please their High Mightinesses to order the college of the Admiralty at Rotterdam, not to allow any more German families to be transported to England. The said memorandum to be inserted here, reading as follows :

"Whereupon, after deliberation, it has been decided to reply to the said Dayrolles that their High Mightinesses cannot prevent those families of the Palatines who already are in this country in order to cross over to England, from being taken thither, but that the Ministers at Cologne and Frankford shall be ordered to warn the people over there not to come this way for that purpose. And a copy of the aforesaid memorandum shall be

---

It affords me no little satisfaction that I am enabled to present a picture of the great gateway and wharf in Rotterdam, known as the Hoofd Port, through which all these emigrants were compelled to pass, and from which, not only these Palatines, but the many thousands more who followed them into the New World, took shipping.

Situated on both sides of the river Maas, 19 miles from its mouth, and 45 miles from Amsterdam, Rotterdam has for centuries been one of the important seaports of Europe. The Rhine, of which the Maas is one of the outlets, gave Rotterdam easy water communication with many important German provinces, and the cantons of Switzerland, and it was at once the most direct as well as natural outlet to the sea, of all the emigrants from that quarter. Even at the present time, from 5000 to 20,000 persons sail annually from its wharfs to this country. For many decades most of the German emigrants took ship at Rotterdam, stopping, however at the little seaport of Cowes, on the isle of Wight, before finally setting sail for America.

This cut was made from an old, and very rare print in the possession of the Pennsylvania Historical Society, which has courteously permitted me to have a fac-simile taken.

THE PENNSYLVANIA-GERMAN SOCIETY.

THE HOOFD-POORT AT ROTTERDAM.

GATEWAY THROUGH WHICH ALL THE GERMAN EMIGRANTS PASSED TO THE WHARF FROM WHICH THEY SAILED FOR AMERICA.

sent to the Presidents, Bilderheecks and Spina and they shall be directed that in case they should learn that more families from the Palatinate or elsewhere intend to come hither in order to cross over to England, to warn the same by such means as shall be deemed fittest, that they shall not be transported thither nor admitted into this country.''

HIGH MIGHTY LORDS.

My Lords : I have had the honor the day before yesterday, to receive your High Mightinesses letter of the 16th inst, with a resolution of the same date attached, taken in pursuance of a memorandum of Secretary Dayrolles. In accordance with the order contained in said resolution, I shall by the fullest means cause all such people who I may learn will go from the Palatinate, or elsewhere, to Holland, in order to cross over to England, to be warned that they cannot be transported to England nor admitted in your High Mightinesses' country.

Tuesday last.

High Mighty Lords
Your High Mightinesses
obedient and faithful servant,
H. VAN BILDERHEECKS.

COLOGNE, Sep. 24, 1709.

HIGH MIGHTY LORDS.

My Lords ; Your High Mightinesses letter and resolution to the memorandum of the Secretary of Her Royal Majesty of Great Britain, taken on the 16th inst., I have with most humble respect duly received by the last mail. I shall not fail to comply therewith and by all fitting means warn such people as intend to go down stream.

But inasmuch as many Dutch Sailors some time since passed though this city to go down stream, who were deprived of everthing and the means which your High Mightinesses are wont to allow to their Ministers for the assistance of destitute ordinary travellers have been exhausted, I do not doubt but your High Mightinesses will have favorably reflected upon my proposition respectfully made to your High Mightinesses Clerk on the 8th inst. and honor me with their resolution, in order that these destitute people may not be left in need, in the severe winter season.

High Mighty Lords

Your High Mightinesses most humble

and most faithful servant,

P. DE SPINA,

Of Margroche.

FRANKFORT, Sept. 26, 1709.

APPENDIX B.

SEVERAL years ago a number of the friends of the Pennsylvania Historical Society raised a large sum of money, —$10,000 I believe— to have transcribed for the use of the Society, the complete manuscript minutes of the Public Record Office of England. These when completed will perhaps reach one hundred large volumes.

Fortunately for my purposes, the volumes covering the year 1709, reached this country while I was engaged in the preparation of this paper, and through the courtesy of Dr. Frederick D. Stone, the Society Librarian, they were placed at my service. Being the daily records of the Board, their accuracy is unimpeachable, and they have enabled me to correct inaccuracies in some of the other contemporary authorities I have consulted. The following extracts will seem to show how embarassing this

German immigration was to the English Government, and also the many schemes that were proposed to shake off the burden.

[F. R. D.]

Journal of the Proceedings of her Majesty's Commissioners for Promoting the trade of this Kingdom, and for inspecting and improving her Plantations in America and elsewhere.

(vol. 21)   WHITEHALL, May the 4th, 1709.

At a meeting of Her Majesty's Commissioners for Trade and Plantations.

Present :

| Earl of Stamford. | Mr. Pulteney. |
| Sr. Ph. Meadows. | Mr. Moncton. |

A letter from the Earl of Sunderland of Yesterday's Date, signifying that some hundreds of poor German Protestants are lately come, and that more are coming from the Palatinate to this Kingdom, and directing this Board to consider of a method for settling the said Germans in some part of this Kingdom, was read. Whereupon ordered that some of the Lutheran ministers in the Savoy have notice to attend the Board to-morrow morning.

WHITEHALL, May 5th, 1709.
Present :

| Earl of Stamford. | Mr. Pulteney. |
| Sr. Ph. Meadows. | Mr. Moncton. |

One of the Lutheran Ministers attending as directed yesterday, and being asked several questions in relation to poor German Protestants Mentioned in Yesterday's Minutes, He said that 300 men, women and children were already come over. That most of them were husbandmen and some few joyners and carpenters : that they are poor and have nothing to subsist on but what is given them in Charity, and are therefore threatened to be turned out of the house they are Lodged in ; he added that there were 700 more of the said Poor Germans now at Rotterdam, who are expected over. And he promised to make a further Enquiry into the Circumstances of these Poor People and give their Lordships an answer thereof, in Writing as soon as Possible.

On May 6th, another letter from the Earl of Sunderland asking the Board to make full inquiry and directions given to write to the Lutheran Minister in the Savoy.

WHITEHALL, May 12th, 1709.
At a meeting of Her Majesty's Commissioners for Trade and Plantations.

Present :

Earl of Stamford.   Mr. Meadows.

Mr. Moncton.

Monsieur Tribekko and Monsieur Ruperti, two of the Lutheran Ministers here, attending in relation to the Poor German Protestants, lately come from the Palatinate, mentioned in the minutes of the 5th instant. They presented to their Lordships, Memorials setting forth the Calamitous condition of these poor People, together with an account of their number, Amounting in all to 852 persons, men, women and children ; their several Trades and Occupations, which were read. And these gentlemen being asked several questions thereupon, they said that several of them had died of want since their coming over. That they had no subsistence left. That they could not speak English, and that therefore none of them had as yet got any business or employment here, but possibly might do it in some time when they had learned the Language. Then being asked further what allowance they thought would be necessary for their present support until some provision could be otherwise made for them, They said they could not readily tell, But would withdraw and as near as Possible make a Calculation thereof ;

and having done the same, they returned and proposed that sixteen pounds per day might be allowed the said 852 Persons for their present support and subsistence : Whereupon a letter to the Earl of Sunderland, signifying the same to his Lordship was drawn up and signed.

———

WHITEHALL, May the 16th, 1709.

At a meeting of Her Majesty's Commissioners for Trade and Plantations :

Present :

Earl of Stamford.   Sr. Ph. Meadows.

Mr. Moncton.

Mr. Ludolph and Justice Chamberlain attending, presented to their Lordships a Memorial, setting forth the reason of the Poor German Protestants coming over to this Kingdom, from the Palatinate, which being read, was returned to them again.

———

WHITEHALL, May 17th, 1709.

At a meeting of Her Majesty's Commissioners for Trade and Plantations.

Present :

Earl of Stamford.   Sr. Ph. Meadows.

Mr. Moncton.

A letter from the Earl of Sunderland of the 15th Instant (in answer to one writ to him on the 12th ditto) Signifying that Her Majesty had given orders for supplying the poor Germans as had been proposed in the said Letter, till they could be otherwise provided for, and that her Majesty was desirous to have the opinion of this Board how such Provision might be made for those Poor people &c was read. Whereupon their Lordships taking the same into consideration, and finding great difficulty in proposing a method to imploy them in such Manner as they may be able to support themselves here. A Letter to the

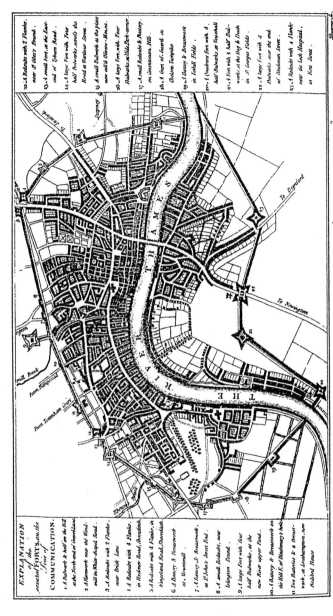

A PLAN of the City and Environs of LONDON, as Fortified by Order of PARLIAMENT, in the Years 1642 & 1643.

London. Published as the Act directs by Alex'r Hogg, at the Kings Arms N°16. Paternoster Row.

Plan of London and surrounding country immediately prior to the Exodus.

Earl of Sunderland acquainting his Lordship therewith and desiring that he would give the Board an opportunity of Conferring with him on that Affair was signed.

Ordered that Mr. Tribekko and Mr. Ruperti, two of the Lutheran Ministers as likewise Mr. Chamberlain and Mr. Ludolph have notice to attend the Board to-morrow morning.

On the following day, May 18, Mr. Tribekko and Mr. Ruperti appeared before the Board. They said that the Tradesmen among them were able to work if they could but find employment. That the Husbandmen might also be provided for if they could but procure work. They believed all who were not sick were capable of working, but the Women and Children could do little else but Spin and Knit. Many of them were from the same county as those who had gone to New York, and were anxious to go there.[1]

At a meeting held on the 21st, Mr. Tribekko presented a list of such as could work. He said 200 of the men (most of them married) were able and fit to work and get a maintenance ; that a Tailor and joiner had got into business ; that 100 women could knit and spin and get a livelihood in that way. As to the rest, they were able to do but little, some being old and infirm ; that they were now in pretty good condition, better accommodated than before.

On May 23, a list of the sick was presented to the Board. They (the Ministers) also gave the Board the unpleasant information that 1300 more of these Germans were come to the country but were still on shipboard, as no place could be found to lodge them. They also informed their Lordships that Her Majesty had been pleased to allow the first 852, £20 per day instead of £16.

---

[1] This allusion evidently refers to the colony led to New York in the previous year by Joshua von Kocherthal.

At a meeting of the Board on May 23, a memorial was presented from the United Governors, Assistants and Society of London for Mines Royal and Balley Works, proposing the employment of such of the poor Germans as are strong and able to labor in the Silver and Copper mines at Penlyn and Merionethshire.

———

WHITEHALL, May 24th, 1709.

At a meeting of Her Majesty's Commissioners for Trade and Plantations.

Present :

Earl of Stamford.   Sr. Ph. Meadows.
Lord Dartmouth.   Mr. Moncton.

A letter from Mr. Taylor inclosing a memorial relating to the Arrival of 1100 more German Protestants from the Palatinate, and that 600 more of them lie at Rotterdam for passage, signifying my Lord Treasurer's desire to know from this Board what is absolutely necessary as well for the 1100 already arrived as the 600 expected from Rotterdam, and how they may most properly be disposed of was read and directions given for Writing an Answer thereto.

Mr. Treke and Mr. Chamberlain attending in relation to the Said Poor People, they acquainted their Lordships that they were still on Shipboard at Woolwich, by reason they had no places provided for them to lodge in. That if tents could be procured, they would take care to Separate the said Germans and place some of them at Greenwich, Lambeth, Fulham and elsewhere, until they could find out work for them, which they hoped to do in a short time. Then being asked if the Ropeyard at Greenwich Should be repaired and fitted up, whether the same would not be convenient for their Accommodation for the present, till they should be otherwise taken care of. They said that the said Ropeyard would be very convenient for a great part of them. Whereupon these Gentlemen were told that their Lordships would give Directions for Writing this Morning to my Lord Treasurer to acquaint him herewith.

May 25, Mr. Tribekko presented a new list to the Board, containing the names of such as were able to work, and such as were not either from Age or Sickness. It contained only 806 names. He said five or six and twenty have died since their arrival. He proposed that £100 should be laid out for flax, iron and steel that the women might be set to spinning and the men employed in making tools for husbandry.

On May 30, the Board instructed the Solicitor General to advise them whether Her Majesty had the right and power to grant parcels of land in her Forests, Chases and Waters in order to convert them to tillage, and also what Security Her Majesty may give to indemnify Parishes for introducing poor families among them.

On June 3, Inquiry was made as to the character of the Society of London for Royal Mines.

WHITEHALL, June 7th, 1709.

At a meeting of Her Majesty's Commissioners for Trade and Plantations.

Present:

Lord Dartmouth.   Sr. Ph. Meadows.

Mr. Moncton.

Mr. Tribekko attending informed their Lordships that 2000 more Poor People were Arrived from the Palatinate in Germany, whereupon he was acquainted that it would be proper for him to present a memorial thereof to a Secretary of State, which he Promised to do accordingly.

Dr. Stringer attended and informed the Lords that the Society (of London for Mines Royal) was incorporated by Queen Elizabeth in the 10th year of her reign. He was requested to produce the seal of incorporation.

WHITEHALL, June 15th, 1709.

At a meeting of Her Majesty's Commissioners for Trade and Plantations.

Present :

Lord Dartmouth.   Sr. Ph. Meadows.

Mr. Moncton.

The proposal of Lord Chamberlain for settling some of the Palatines in Staffordshire and Gloucestershire was considered. He had great parcels of land in these counties which were waste of which he could grant to each family a sufficient amount for the term of three years, they paying a penny an acre. That he would at once take 20 or 25 families. That they should have timber and lime with the lands for building, but he hoped the Queen would be at the charge of erecting the cottages and subsist them until they were in a condition to help themselves.

On the 21 fresh proposals were considered from Lord Chamberlain. They declined his offer and said to accept of it and settle all the Germans would cost £150.000. That the idea was not to put them on a better footing than British subjects, but merely to aid them until they could help themselves. These Settlers would benefit his Lordship's estate, as he could retain them as tenants. Her Majesty could only be at the charge of conveying them there.

On June 23, Mr. Tribekko presented a memorial to the Board that there had been a great increase in the number of the Palatines, and they could not be taken care of without greater assistance, and asking for the same.

A memorial was also read from Dr. Stringer and others about employing the Palatines in some mines in Wales and elsewhere.

A warrant from her Majesty dated June 4, 1709, calling for £24 daily to the Germans was over and above the £16 per day, was read. Also another of the 14th calling for the payment of £40 daily.

A proposal was made to settle 200 families in the island of Jamaica, but the planters objected, as they were required to send some of their negroes to make a preparatory settlement for the Germans.

On August 8th, the Board discussed the speedy settlement of the Palatines so as to put an end to the heavy expense of their subsistence. It was resolved to give special encouragement to persons and parishes as should be willing to receive any of these poor Palatines. It was agreed to allow each parish £5 per head for such care, the Queen to be at the charge of sending them to their respective places.

On August 17th, Colonel Laws advocated before the Board, the sending of a colony of Germans to Jamaica. There were, he said, 40,000 negroes there and not above 2,500 whites. There was much unsettled land, enough for 50,000 families.

This Jamaica Settlement was discussed at almost every meeting of the Board but nothing ever came of it.

Lord Carbury also had great tracts of lands on which he offered to colonize some of the Germans, but he asked £5 per acre which was deemed excessive. Later however, he made a more liberal offer which was discussed at further meetings of the Board, but there is no record that any ultimate arrangement of this kind was made with him.[2]

---

[2] Records of the Board of Trade.

APPENDIX C.

A BRIEF FOR THE COLLECTION OF MONEY ASKED FOR, AND
GRANTED BY THE QUEEN.

TO THE QUEEN'S MOST EXCELLENT MAJESTY.

ARMS OF CHUR-SACHSEN.

THE Humble Petition of your Majesties, Justices of Peace for the County of Middlesex, held at Hick's Hall, June 7, 1709 *Showeth*,

That being inform'd that several Thousand *Germans* of the *Protestant* Religion, oppressed by Exactions of the *French* in their own Country, have fled for Refuge into this your Majesty's Kingdom of *Great Britain*; who must have perished, had not your Majestie's Generous and Seasonable Bounty subsisted them; and being sensible that they labor still under great Wants, and stand in need of farther Relief for their Subsistence, do therefore crave leave to offer your Majesty our Humble Opinion, That a

Brief for the Collection of the Charity of all well disposed Persons, in all Churches and Meetings, and otherwise within this County, as soon as your Majesty shall think fit to grant it ; will be effectual to Raise a considerable Sum for their present Relief. All of which we Humbly submit to your Majesties great Wisdom ; and we shall, as in Duty bound, ever Pray.

AT THE COURT OF ST. JAMES'S, JUNE 16, 1709. PRESENT THE QUEEN'S MOST EXCELLENT MAJESTY IN COUNCIL.

Upon Reading this Day at the Board the Humble Petition of the Justices of Peace for the County of *Middlesex*, at the general Sessions of Peace for the said County ; representing to her Majesty, the great Wants and Necessities of several Thousand *Germans* of the *Protestant* Religion, who being oppressed by the Exactions of the *French* in their own Country, have fled for Refuge into this Kingdom, and must have perished, had not her Majesty's Generous and Seasonable Bounty reliev'd them : And humbly offering that for their further Relief and subsistence, a Brief may be Issued for the Collection of the Charity of well disposed Persons within the said County. Her Majesty out of her tender Regard and Compassion to these Poor People, is pleased to condescend thereunto, and to order that the Right Honorable, the Lord High Chancellor of Great Britain do cause Letters Patents to be prepared, and passed under the Great Seal for that Purpose, &c.

Accordingly, a Brief has been Granted by Her Majesty for the Relief, Subsistence and Settlement of the Poor Distressed *Palatines*, to this Effect.

THE BRIEF.

Whereas by reason of the many great Hardships and Oppressions which the People of the Palatinate, near the Rhine, in Germany, (more especially the Protestants) have sustained and lain under for several Years past, by the frequent Invasions and repeated Inroads of the French, (whereby more than Two

Thousand of their greatest Cities, Market Towns and Villages) have been burnt down to the Ground ; as Heidelburg, Manheim, Worms, Spire, Frankendale, and other Towns ; and great Numbers have perished in Woods, and Caves, by Hunger, Cold and Nakedness, Several Thousands have been forced to leave their Native Country, and seek Refuge in other Nations ; and of them near Eight Thousand Men, Women and Children, are come, and are now in and near the City of London, in a very poor and miserable Condition. And whereas it hath been humbly Represented unto us, as well by an Address of our Justices of the Peace for the County of Middlesex, at their General Session of the Peace, held at Hick's Hall as by others (of) our Loving Subjects, on the behalf of the said Poor Palatines : That Notwithstanding our Bounty allowed to them, without which they must have perished ; yet they still labor under great wants, and stand in need of further Relief for their Subsistence and Settlement, in such manner that they may not only support themselves, but be rendered capable of Advancing the Wealth and Strength of our Nation, in regard they are naturally of a strong, healthful Constitution, inur'd to Labor and Industry, and great part of them to Husbandry ; therefore the said Justices, and our other Loving Subjects, on behalf of the said Poor Distressed Palatines, have humbly besought us to Grant unto the said Poor Palatines, our Gracious Letters Patents, License and Protection, under our Great Seal of Great Britain, to impower them to Ask, Collect and Receive, the Alms and Benevolence of all our Loving Subjects, throughout that part of our Kingdom of Great Britain called England, Dominion of Wales and Town of Berwick upon Tweed, UNTO which humble Request we have Graciously conde-scended, not doubting but when these Presents shall be made known unto our Loving Subjects, they will readily and cheer-fully contribute to the Relief and Support of the said poor Distressed Palatines : considering them as Brethren, and Sym-pathizing with them in this their Miserable State and Condi-tion.

KNOW YE THEREFORE, that of our Special Grace and Princely Compassion, we have Given and Granted to the said poor Palatines, and to their Deputy or Deputies, the Bearer and Bearers thereof : full Power, License and authority to Ask, Collect and Receive the Alms and Charitable Benevolence of our Loving Subjects ; Not only Householders, but also Servants, Strangers, Lodgers, and others in all the Cities, Towns, Villages, &c., In our kingdom of England, &c. We likewise purposing to cause the like License and Authority to be granted in Relation to our Loving Subjects in Scotland. And we do require all Parsons, Vicars, Curates, Teachers and Preachers of every Separate Congregation, to read the said Brief in their Several Churches and Congregations, and earnestly to exhort their Auditors to a liberal Contribution of their Charity to the said Poor Palatines : and that the Minister and Church Warden of every Parish, shall go from House to House to Ask and Receive from their Parishioners their Christian and Charitable Contributions.

And we do hereby Authorize and Appoint the Lord Archbishop of Canterbury, the Lord High Chancellor, Lord High Treasurer, &c. (with a great number of our Lords Spiritual and Temporal, Knights, Gentlemen, &c.,) To be Trustees and Receivers of the said Charity, &c. And to dispose and Distribute the Money which shall be Collected, in such manner as shall be found Necessary and Convenient for the better Employment and Settlement of the said Poor Palatines, by making Contracts in their behalf or by any other Lawful Means and Ways whatsoever, &c.

In Pursuance of this Brief the Following Order was Published:

WHITE HALL, July 20th, 1709.

By Order of the Right Honorable, the Lords and others, her Majesties Commissioners for Receiving and Disposing of the Money to be Collected for the Subsistence and Settlement of the poor Palatines : Notice is hereby given, that they will hold their General Meeting at Doctors Commons every Wednesday at Four in the Afternoon. Notice is hereby likewise given, that the said Commissioners are come to a Resolution for disposing and settling as many of the said Palatines as conveniently they can, in North Britain and Ireland, and the Plantations, and that they will at their Committee receive Proposals in order thereunto.

Notice is likewise given, that any Masters of Ships, Trading in the coal, or other Coast Trade, are at liberty to employ such of the said Palatines, as are willing to serve them on Board such ships ; and that such Masters may apply themselves to a Person Appointed to attend at the several Places where the said Palatines now are for that Purpose.[3]

The Persons appointed Commissioners and Trustees by the said Letters Patent, were :

The Lord Archbishop of Canterbury.
Lord High Chancellor of Great Britain.
Lord High Treasurer of Great Britain.
John, Lord Somers, Lord President of the Council.
John, Duke of Newcastle, Lord Privy Seal.
William, Duke of Devonshire, Steward of the Household.
Charles, Duke of Somerset, Master of the Horse.
James, Duke of Ormund.
Wriothesly, Duke of Bedford.
John, Duke of Buckingham and Normandy.
James, Duke of Queensbury and Dover, Secretary of State.
Henry, Marquis of Kent, Chamberlain of the Household.
Evelyn, Marquis of Dorchester.
Thomas, Earl of Pembroke and Montgomery, Lord High Admiral of Great Britain.
James, Earl of Derby.
Thomas, Earl of Stamford.

---

[3] State of the Palatines.

THE PENNSYLVANIA-GERMAN SOCIETY.

A STREET SCENE IN LONDON IN 1709.

FROM A CONTEMPORARY PRINT.

Charles, Earl of Sunderland, Secretary of State.

Lawrence, Earl of Rochester.

Henry, Lord Bishop of London.

Thomas, Lord Bishop of Rochester.

Jonathan, Lord Bishop of Winchester.

John, Lord Bishop of Ely.

William, Lord Bishop of Lincoln.

William, Lord Dartmouth.

Charles, Lord Halifax.

The Right Honorable Mr. Secretary Boyle.

James Vernon, Esq.

Lord Chief Justice Holt.

Sir John Trevor, Master of the Rolls.

Lord Chief Justice Trevor.

Sir Charles Hedges.

John Smith, Esq., Chancellor of the Exchequer.

Sir James Montague, Knight, Attorney General.

Robert Eyre, Esq., Solicitor General.

The Lord Mayor, Aldermen, Recorder, and Sheriffs of the
city of London.

The Honorable Spencer Compton, Esq.

The Honorable George Watson, Esq.

Sir Matthew Dudley.

Sir John Bucknall.

Sir John Stanley.

Sir Henry Furnace.

Sir John Phillips, Bart.

Sir Alexander Cairns, Bart.

Sir Theodore Janssen.

Sir James Collett.

Sir Edmund Harrison.

Sir William Scawen, Knight.

Sir John Elwill, Knight.

Dr. Willis, Dean of Lincoln.

Dr. White Kennet, Dean of Peterborough.

Dr.——Godolphin, Dean of St. Pauls.

Dr. Thomas Manningham, Dean of Windsor.
Dr. Thomas Bray.
Dr. George Smallridge.
Dr. Moss.
Dr. Bradford.
Dr. Butler.
Dr. Linford.
Dr. Pelling.
The Rev. Samuel Clerk.
Conradus Wornley.
Ulrich Scherer.
John Tribekko and Andrew Ruperty, Clerks.
Samuel Travers, Esq., Surveyor General.
John Plumer.
John Shute.
Joseph Offley.
Richard Walaston.
David Hexsteter.
John Ward.
Henry Cornish.
Nathaniel Gould.
Justus Beck.
John Dolben.
Richard Marten.
Arthur Bailey.
Micaija Perry.
Henry Martin.
William Dudley.
George Townsend.
Thomas Railton.
Ralph Bucknal.
John Chamberlayne.
William Dawson, Esq.
Francis Eyles, Esq.
Frederick Slare, Doctor of Physic.
James Keith, Doctor of Physic.

Thomas Smith, Esq.
Robert Hales.
Henry William Ludolph.
Robert de Neuvillic.
Peter Foy.
William Falkener.
Henry Hoar.
Walter Cock, Gent.
Jonathan James, Gent.[4]

---

[4] Palatine Refugees in England, pp. 35-36.

APPENDIX D.

[The passage of a Naturalization act by Great Britain early in the Spring of 1709, was not lost upon Holland. That country had been benefitted to an almost inconceivable degree by the Huguenot refugees who were driven out of France by the revocation of the Edict of Nantes, many of whom had settled themselves in the Low Countries. When, therefore, Holland again saw these thousands of industrious men, farmers and handicraftmen, invited to become citizens of Great Britain, she also passed a naturalization act in the hope they might be induced to tarry in the Netherlands. The following is the proclamation which was issued on June 24, 1709, by the States of Holland and West Fries land, for the general naturalization of Protestants. F. R. D.

HOLLAND'S NATURALIZATION ACT.

ARMS OF AMSTERDAM.

𝒯HE States of Holland and West Friesland, to all who shall hear and see these Presents, Greeting : We make it known that having taken into consideration that the Grandeur and Prosperity of a country does not in general consist of the Multitude of Inhabitants and that in particular this Prince is increased in Power and Riches by the Concourse of unhappy and dispersed Persons

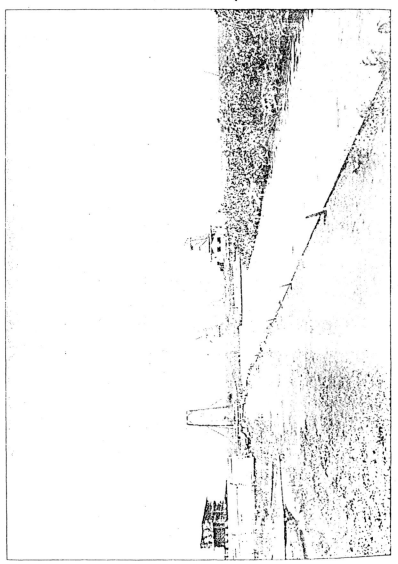

A VIEW IN HOLLAND.

who being driven from their own Country for the Profession of
the True Reformed Religion, or other oppressions, have taken
sanctity in this Province, and have a long time since contributed
to the increase of Trade and Public Wealth. That beside the
Refugees, who left France upon account of their Religion and
have already lived a considerable time in this Country, have
rendered themselves worthy of the favorable attention of the
Regency for their Persons and Families, and consequently
ought to enjoy their General Protection as the other Inhabitants.

For these causes We have thought fit to Order and Decree
as we Order and Decree by these Presents, that all persons who
have withdrawn themselves out of the Kindgom of France, or
other Countries, for the Profession of the true Reformed Religion, and have taken Sanctuary in this Province of Holland
and West Friesland, and settled themselves therein, and likewise the Children of the said persons whom they brought with
them, or were born in the Said Province, as also all other such
Refugees, who for the future shall either directly out of France
or other Countries, take Refuge in this Province and close
their Abode therein shall be received and acknowledged, as we
do receive and acknowledge them by these Presents, for our
Subjects, and Natives of our country of Holland and West
Friesland, and by virtue thereof shall enjoy for the future
Privilege and Prerogatives that our other Natural Born Subjects
enjoy, as such of them belonging ; and that in consequence
thereof they shall enjoy the Rights of Naturalization according
to the Resolution bearing the date of Sept. 25, 1670. That
therefore all these who will take the Benefit of this our Favor
shall apply personally to the President or Commissioner of the
Court ; under whose jurisdiction they are, or to Magistrates or
Town Baliffs and Judges of Villages where they are settled, or
intend to chose their Abode, who after a short Examination, to
know whether the Said Persons are truly Refugees, as aforesaid, shall Register their Names, that the same may appear
forever. And that this may be known to everybody, we

require these presents to be Published and Affixed and Executed in the usual manner.

Done at the Hague, July 18, 1709.

SIMON VAN BEAUMONT.

APPENDIX E.

THE PALATINATE.

BRIEF SKETCH OF THE POLITICAL HISTORY OF THE COUNTRY FROM
THE ELEVENTH TO THE EIGHTEENTH CENTURY, DRAWN FROM
VARIOUS SOURCES.

[Few names are more familiar to persons of average culture than *The Palatinate*, used in a geographical sense. Every one of German origin has heard it repeated again and again as a household term, and yet how many, even among those who are reckoned as scholarly men know more about it than that it was a German province and famous for the sufferings of its people during the seventeenth century, as the varying fortunes of war made them the victims alike of victor and vanquished? Inasmuch as by far the greatest number of those who went to England in 1709 came from the Palatinate, and as it was for more than half a century afterward one of the main sources of the German emigration to Pennsylvania, a more general account of this historic land will not be inappropriate here.   F. R. D.]

ARMS OF THE CHUR-PFALTZ.

HE two territorial divisions known as the Upper and Lower Palatinate, had a separate existence as early as the 11th century. At that time they, along with the duchy of Souabia, the duchy of Franconia, the palatinate of Burgundy west of Mount Jura, the province of Egra and other fiefs in Switzerland, the Tyrol and elsewhere, composed the possessions of the imperial dynasty of Hohenstaufen, which took its name from a high conical mountain—*der hohe Staufen*—in the valley of the Rems, in Soubia. There Frederick of Büren, the founder of the family, had built a mighty castle, the home of his chivalrous race. He married Agnes, daughter of Henry IV, Emperor of Germany, and she brought him the duchy of Soubia as a dower. For nearly 200 years the Hohenstaufens held sway. The last of the name, Conradin, wasted his heritage in his Italian campaigns and perished on the scaffold at Naples in 1268. The duchy of Franconia was dismembered. This Palatinate which formed a part of it fell into the hands of new owners.

The Palatinate comprised two separate provinces, which were divided from each other by the secular and ecclesiastical state of Franconia. First was the Palatinate on the Rhine, or Lower Palatinate—*Pfalz am Rhein*—situated on both sides of that River, and bounded by Würtemburg, Baden, Alsace, Lorraine, Treves and Hesse. It contained 2288 square miles and to-day contains about 700,000 inhabitants. The Upper Palatinate, or *Ober-Pfalz* on the east was surrounded by Bohemia, Bavaria and Nurnburg. The Upper Palatinate contains 3845 square miles and about 550,000 souls.

The Emperor Frederick II gave the Palatinate to Louis of Bavaria and it remained a part of that country until 1329, when the Emperor Louis IV in the treaty of Pavia conferred it on the sons and relatives of his brother. The Electoral dignity was alternately exercised by the Duke of Bavaria and the holders of the Rheinish Palatinate, because the electoral dignity was attached to the Rhein Pfalz, whose court was invested with the judiciary power of the empire in case of the absence of the Emperor. Though divided into four lines, the Palatinate was nevertheless considered as a united State. These lines were as follows : First the Electorate on the Rhine,—*Kur-Rhein*. Second, Sulzbach, or *Upper Palatinate*, established by Count John. Third, Simmern, with the counties of Veldenz and

Spa.iheim, on the Rhine, north of the Electorate. Fourth, Mossbach, on the Neckar, in Souabia.

In the Golden Bull issued by the Emperor Charles IV, in 1356, all the rights and privileges which the great vassals of the empire had usurped, were conceded to them. The electors were seven in number, ranking in the following order : I. the Archbishop of Mayence, as Arch Chancellor of Germany, II. the Archbishop of Treves, as Arch Chancellor of Burgundy. III. the Archbishop of Cologne, as Arch Chancellor of Italy. IV. The King of Bohemia, as Arch Seneschal. V. the Count Palatine, as Arch-Sewer, VI. the Duke of Saxe Wittenberg as Arch Marshal, and VII. the Margrave of Brandenburg. These territories were considered inalienable feudal possessions of the Empire.

Coming down to a more recent period we find the electorate in the hands of Frederick III, in 1559, who introduced Calvinism, and gave his protection to the Huguenots. He maintained the Reformed religion with extreme severity throughout his electorate. Sylvan, a Socinian clergyman who would admit of but one person in the Godhead, was beheaded by his order in 1572. His son Louis, who was a zealous Lutheran, tried to undo all his father's work. On entering his Capital, Heidelberg, he ordered all of his subjects who were not Lutherans to leave the city. The Calvinist preachers who refused to recant, were expelled the country. From this time on the people of the Palatinate were frequently compelled to change their religion to comform with the tenets of the ruling princes, being successively Catholic, Calvinistic, Lutheran, Calvinistic and again Lutheran.

Ludevick V lost his electorate in 1623 to his kinsman the Duke of Bavaria. The latter retained the Upper Palatinate and the electoral dignity, but in 1648 the Rheinish Palatinate was conveyed to Frederick's son, and the VIII. electorate created for him. During the war of the Spanish Succession, in 1694, the Elector again revived the Upper Palatinate, and all the ancient rights resumed again by Bavaria after the war. During these numerous changes the Palatinate was cruelly desolated by the armies that from motives of conquest and religion overran her soil.   In 1801 France seized all on the west bank of the Rhine, and divided the remainder between Bavaria, Nassau and Hesse Darmstadt.   In 1815 the left bank was restored to Germany, the greater part of the Lower Palatinate being given to Bavaria ; Prussia got the Rhine Province, Hesse Starkenburg and Rhine Hesse, while Baden received Manheim, Heidelberg and Mossback. [4a]

OFFICIAL TITLES OF THE ELECTOR. [5]

The Elector Palatine's titles are : By the Grace of God, Count Palatine of the Rhine, Arch-Treasurer and Elector of the Empire, Duke of Bavaria, Juliers, Cleves and Berg ; Count of Veldentz, Spanheim, Marck, Ravensburg and Mœurs, Lord of Ravenstein, &c., &c.

Frederick the IV marry'd Louisa Julia of Orange, had great quarrels with the House of Austria about Religion and dy'd Anno Dom 1610.   His Son and Successor, Frederick the Vth, marry'd Elizabeth, Daughter of James the Ist, of Great Britain, Succeeded to his Fathers Quarrels with the House of Austria about Religion, and was chosen King of Bohemia ; but for want of being duly supported, was defeated at the Battel of Prague ; after which he lost both his Crown and his Dominions. He had Issue the illustrious Princess *Sophia*, born in 1630 ; marry'd *Earnest Augustus*, Duke of *Hanover*, who is now Electress Dowager, Mother to the present Elector, presumptive Heiress to the Crowns of *Great Britain* and *Ireland*, and as

---

[4a] The principal authorities consulted in preparing this brief sketch were *Koeppen's Middle Ages, Chambers Cyclopedia* and *Menzel's Germany.*

[5] Palatine Refugees in England, p. 21.

Map of the Palatinate at the close of the 17th Century.

illustrious for her excellent Qualities, as for her high birth. [6]
Frederick the V was succeeded by his Son, *Charles Louis*, who
by the Treaty of Westphalia was restor'd to the Lower Pala-
tinate, and the Electoral Dignity. He was a pious and learned
Prince, and dy'd in 1680. His son *Charles* succeeded, was
Elector of this Line, and dy'd without Issue in 1685. The
present Elector is (by failure of the fore-mention'd Line) of
the Branch of *Newburgh*, of the Family of *Deux Ponts*. The
Majority of the People are Protestants, who have been much
discourag'd since the Succession of the Duke of *Newburgh*, a
Papist, to the Electorate, and by the *barbarous* Invasions of the
French.[7]

ANOTHER ACCOUNT OF THE PALATINATE AND ITS RULERS,
TOGETHER WITH SOME OF ITS POLITICAL VICISSI-
TUDES IN THE LATTER HALF OF THE
SEVENTEENTH CENTURY.

The Poor Palatines who are the objects of our present
Charity, inhabited lately a Principality in Germany called the
Palatinate, which is divided into the Upper and Lower Palatinate : the Upper belonging to the Duke of Bavaria, according
to the Treaty of Munster and the Lower to the Count Palatine
of the Rhine, who formerly enjoyed the whole. The Countrey
takes its name from the Office of Count Palatine, bestowed
by the Emperor on those who administered Justice in his Name
to the Empire ; of which there were two, one on the Rhine, who
had the Charge of Franconia, and the neighboring Countreys,
and the other in Saxony and other Countreys subject to the
Saxony law. Hence it is that the Electors of Saxony and

---

[6] Sophia, the granddaughter of James I, the youngest of thirteen children, was born on October 13, 1630. As stated above she was declared
by Parliament to be entitled to the succession after the death of Queen
Anne. She did not attain the crown. She died on June 8, 1714. She
was the mother of George I, who was proclaimed King of Great
Britain immediately upon the death of Queen Anne on August 1, 1714.

[7] Palatine Refugees in England, pp. 21-22.

the Elector Palatine or the Elector of Bavaria are Vicars of the Empire in their respective Provinces, when there is an interregnum by the Emperor's death or otherwise. At first the Count Valentine of the Rhine had no possessions on that River, but in Process of Time, got them by Marriage, Purchase or Imperial Gift, and formed a very considerable Principality. In 1576 the Elector Frederick III began to entertain many Protestant Families at Frankendale, who fled from the Low Countries. His Successors doing the like in other Towns, did thereby mightily enrich that Country. This Prince made his Revenue very considerable by taking away the Church Lands upon the Change of Religion ; by his Right of conducting Strangers whom he obliged to make use of his Guards, not only in his own Territories, but in the neighboring Bishopricks, and Earldoms, and by Toll upon Merchandize that passes his Dominions, and the Title he has to the Goods of Strangers, or of those who came to Settle without express leave, in the Palatinate.

Frederick III was succeeded by his son, Lewis IV, who turned Protestant, and was succeeded by Frederick IV, who abandoned Popery. He married Louise, daughter of the Prince of Orange, by whom he had Frederick V, who was chosen King of Bohemia, but who by the loss of a great Battle at Prague, and the Supineness of the English Court, who ought to have assisted him, he marrying Elizabeth, Daughter to King James I, he was obliged to abandon his Countrey. He died at Mentz in 1632, leaving him Three Sons, Charles, Lewis, Robert or Rupert, and Edward. Prince Rupert lived in England, and died without Legitimate Issue. Edward left Three Daughters; one named Sophia, married to the Duke of Hanover, and is now alive, and declared by act of Parliament the next Protestant Succession to the Crown of England, after the Decease of our Most Gracious Queen Anne, whom God grant long to Reign. Charles succeeded his Father Frederick V in the Electorate Palatine, and married Charlotte, Daughter of the Landgrave of Hesse Castle, by whom he had Charles and Elizabeth Charlott. She was married to the Duke of Orleans, only Brother to the present French King, (Louis XIV) in 1687. It was reported at that time that King Louis having by Treaty of Marriage allowed that Princess, who was a Protestant, the Liberty to use her own Religion, yet when she came to the Frontiers of that Kingdom, on her way to Paris, to consummate her Marriage, that faithless King sent her a Peremptory Message that she should proceed no farther unless she would renounce the Protestant Religion. Whereupon the unhappy Prince, her Father, who was afraid to incur his Anger, consented thereto[8] to save his Dominions from Destruction ; but in a Year or Two after upon some unjust Pretence, he sent the Dauphin, his Son, with a great Army into that Countrey, who ruined it in the most Deplorable Manner that was ever heard of.

Charles succeeded his Father in the Electorate, and William, Duke of Newburg, a Roman Catholic, is the present Elector Palatine.

To show how the Palatinate was overrun by the fierce Soldiery of different nations the following brief statement may be quoted :

The City of Philipsburg, reckon'd the first in the Palatinate, has been taken six times ; viz. in 1633, by the Imperialists, the Year After by the Swedes, and in 1636, by the Imperialists, in 1644 by the Duke d' Enghien, afterwards Prince of Conde, by the Germans in 1676, and by the Dauphin on his Birth Day, the 1st of November, 1688, but was restor'd to the Empire by the Treaty of Ryswick.[9]

---

[8] State of the Palatines, pp. 3-4.
[9] Palatine Refugees in England, p. 26.

APPENDIX F.

ARMS OF PENN, FROM THF FIRST
PROVINCIAL CURRENCY
PRINTED 1723.

I AVAIL myself of this opportunity to express my sincere thanks to my good friend, Hon. Samuel W. Pennypacker, of the Philadelphia Court of Common Pleas, for the loan of an extremely rare and most curious and valuable little book, published in 1711, a fac-simile of the title-page of which is reproduced on page 389. Chapter VI of this rare volume gives what purports to be a detailed account of the exact number of these German emigrants, their daily life in London and elsewhere in England, their places of residence, the regulations of their several camps, their treatment by the English Government and populace, the efforts to settle them throughout the United Kingdoms and elsewhere and their final disposition. So interesting have I found all these details that I have translated the entire chapter and present it herewith.

The name of the writer of this account is, I believe, unknown ; but whoever he may have been, and his barbarous German does not indicate a man of much culture, he evidently was personally on the spot at the time, and had actual knowledge of much that he relates. There is no reason to doubt so much of his narrative as came under his own observation; but my investigations among other and as I believe unquestionable contemporary sources of information have satisfied me that he greatly although unintentionally no doubt, exaggerates the number of these German arrivals. The amount of money raised by public subscriptions, and the sums appropriated from time to time from the English Treasury and applied to the relief of these strangers are on record. It is also in evidence among how many persons these monies were distributed. The number does not reach one half those given by our author. Official documents must be given credence as against the statements of a narrator who presents us with his unsupported account only. In fact, another writer, a contemporary, whose account is printed in this same book and next to this account, sets down the number at less than one half that given in this chapter. It also is very specific, and pretends to give even the nationality of all these emigrants. It will be found in Appendix H.

I incline to the opinion that this is the original source of the statement that these Germans in London, in 1709, numbered more than 33,000 souls, found in Löher, Rupp, Fisher and other writers, all of whom have made the assertion without indicating the sources of their information. Löher was perhaps the first to copy it, and all the rest followed him blindly. This unknown writer's narrative is, however, the fullest and most minute of any I have found, and is marvelously interesting despite his uneven temper and frequent contradictory statements. I may add that I believe this is the first time this narrative has been given to the public in the English language.

F. R. D.

CHAPTER VI.

"BEING A SHORT ACCOUNT OF THOSE GERMANS WHO, AS IT
WERE THROUGH SOME SPECIES OF ENCHANTMENT, IN 1709,
SAILED OVER THE SEA INTO ENGLAND. HOW IT FARED
WITH THEM, WHEN THEY ARRIVED AND WHERE THEY
AFTERWARDS TOOK UP THEIR ABODE."

HANSEATIC ARMS.
(LONDON.)

IN order not to detain the courteous reader with a tedious and unpleasant narration, I will briefly refer to the things which were done openly in England, before the "Præludia," before the arrival of the Germans in 1708, on Blackheath. On the 24-25-26-27 and 28 days of July, 1708, not only in the gloomy night, but also in broad daylight, many things were witnessed by all four camps whereon the following year, the Germans camped on the Black Head or "Blackheath," namely upon the Ritter-Kamm, and in the "Camberwell," and in the Middle camp, just like a well laid off military encampment, many thousands of people, or divers kinds, and religiously educated, saw the spectacle with their own eyes, and to which they have solemnly attested, and have related to the minutest details, all the circumstances worthy of belief.

Among others, there was one witness, deep rooted in the faith, Jaun Alplin, minister of Capella College, near Grinovium and also Mr. John Burian, minister in the church of Dertforth not yet knowing what significance should come out of this. In appearance, it has become cause for higher admiration and

Das verlangte / nicht erlangte Canaan bey den Lust-Gräbern;

Oder

Ausführliche Beschreibung

Von der unglücklichen Reise derer jüngsthin aus Teutschland nach dem
Engelländischen in America gelegenen

Carolina und Pensylvanien

wallenden Pilgrim / absonderlich dem einseitigen übelgegründeten

Kochenthalersschen Bericht

wohlbedächtig jutgegen geletzt

Jn

I. Einem Beantwortungs-Schreiben etlicher dieß
Sach angehenden Fragen ; nebst einer Vorrede Morit Wilhelm Höens.

II. Ermahnungs-Schreiben an die bereits dahin
verreißte Teutsche / Anthon Wilhelm Böhmens.

III. Der Berg-Predigt Christi / und Gebettern vor
die noch dahin auf dem Weg begriffenen 2c.

IV. Königl. Englischen deswegen nach Teutschland
erlassenen Abmahnung.

V. Kurtzen Relation, jener dabey erlittenen Elendes
und Schicksals.

VI. Noch einer andern Relation davon.

VII. Einem Stück der Warnungs-Predigt von
Hn. Johann Tribeck, 2c. den zurückreisenden
in Londen gehalten.

Alles aus Liebe zur Wahrheit und patriotischem Wohlmeinen
zusammen verfasset.

Franckfurt und Leipzig / M DCC XI.

390 The German Exodus to England in 1709.

greater confusion, that in the presence of those encamping, especially those on the Blackheath, many thousands of white birds like doves, gathered, and after they had flown about in the sky for a few days, they died there and were buried by those that were left, in the cool sand. Thereupon the Englishmen ventured all sorts of conjectures and waited ever after for a fulfillment of their conjectures.

Finally in the year never to return, 1709, on the 6th and 8th of May, eleven ships filled with Germans arrived in the great and mighty city of London, in the neighborhood of St. Catharine's and the Royal Brewery, and there landed from them 18,006 persons, old men, young men and women, who after being sent to Blackheath, where the camp was laid out as before stated by the direction of the Queen, were ordered to lodge four by four in the tents provided for them.

A fortnight before the already named eleven ships arrived, five others had come bringing 4324 persons, transported from Holland to England, who also betook themselves to the camping place where they were kindly received by a nobleman through the gracious commands of the Queen. On St. John's Day four more ships arrived under full sail bringing 2138 souls, among whom were two clerical gentlemen, one named Master George Hainer, formerly vicar at Holtzen and Rudling, in the dominion of Lansenberg, and of the Evangelical Lutheran re-, ligion; the other was John Stager, a Reformed student from Nassau Siegen. He believed these 2138 were more highly regarded than any of the rest of the Germans, because they brought no Catholics with them, but at the command of their religious leaders debarred them from the ships. On this account they also received the best tents and the most pleasant location in the camp, ·namely the Rittercamp, and a more gracious eye was cast upon them than upon the others, by the wise Queen and the Parliament.

Six weeks after this three ships arrived in Greenwich haven with 1328 Germans, who had to go into the Middle camp by the wholesale, because they looked somewhat slovenly and had a good many Catholics among them.

About eight days before Michaelmas, (Sep. 29) the number of Germans was again increased by 4003 souls, part of whom took up their march at once into Ireland, partly because it was becoming colder. (We have not taken into account the 3060 men, women and children who were buried at Blackheath.) They were in the meantime lodged in St. Catharine's and in the Royal Brewery. At last, three days before St. Martin's Day, (Nov. 11) the camp was removed. The beginning was made with the Rittercamp, because the Lord Commissioners had sought out the best lodgments for them. More than one hundred wagons were sent to take our beggarly property from the camp, so that none had to work or incur expense. For eight days we had to take up our quarters in the Redhouse, until the rooms at Charles Cox's warehouse were cleaned. During the following eight days, while we were standing outside the Rittercamp at the Redhouse, two other ships arrived with 945 souls, who were at once directed to take up winter quarters in the above named warehouse.

Two ships were driven out of their course by a storm and these did not arrive until the second Sunday in Advent, and then only with 540 persons. The above named were sent to Westforth in order to have good quarters and not to further suffer as they had already done on the sea. In the Christmas week there was a report that some of the very richest men in Germany came to England, but in truth they were only corrupted Swiss and a few from Nassau Siegen. They had a few old horses, which I believe they would have eaten because of their great hunger.

There were 288 souls scattered about the streets by the Tower, where 168 large pieces of cannon were placed, which, as was customary, were fired when ships coming across the sea, arrived in the harbor.

At New Year 72 souls came over land about 100 miles, they having been deceived and brought hither on Holland coal ships.

After these there arrived by packet boat at one time 20, at

another 30, now more, now less, until the total number of Germans was 32,468 souls.

In order that I may take up again my former thought, I desire to inform the reader how it fared with the rest of these in camp in the taking up of winter quarters. First, the Catholics in the remaining camps were separated from the Lutherans and Reformed, and for a few days they were encamped by themselves. Then the gracious will of the Queen was made known to them. If they would enter the Protestant fold, they would secure the royal favor and protection, but if they decided to cling to their idolatrous religion, they might as well make up their minds to return to the Fatherland at once. They should have their free-will in the matter, because, inasmuch as the English people were alarmed at the growth of the Papacy, they were obliged to be on their guard lest it should get too much power; they could hardly do otherwise. Whereupon 3584 Catholics resolved to return to their homes again. After this resolution was made known, each of these persons received ten Reichs guelden as expense money on their way, and were placed on eight ships that they might be carried to Holland. The 520 Catholics who remained in England, became Protestant; 322 becoming Lutherans and the rest Reformed.

After this separation, the Middle camp also broke up and moved into the Redhouse, where the first ones had just quitted their quarters and sailed on the Thames to Battle Bridge to the warehouse of Mr. Charles Cox, with all their property. It was indeed a most excellent opportunity to pick out the Germans among them. The above named camp on Blackheath followed the Middle one into the Redhouse and then there were in all 17,000 souls to spend the winter together. In order that they might get along well, an overseer selected from their number belonging to a noble German family was given complete authority over them. He was made a general sanitary inspector and supervisor of the cooking booth.

Continuous envy and contention arose among the women while cooking. One would say to another in a threatening tone,

Kirchen-Ordnung/

Der Chriſtlichen und der ungeänderten
Augſpurgiſchen Confeſſion
Zugethanen
Gemeinde in LONDON,
Welche,
Durch Göttliche Verleyhung,
Im 1694. Jahre,
Am 19. Sonntage nach dem Feſt der Heiligen
Dreyfaltigkeit,
Solenniter eingeweyhet und eingeſegnet
worden,
In St. Mary s Savoy.

Ep. 1. Cor. 14. v. 33. 40.
GOtt iſt nicht ein GOtt der Unordnung, ſondern des
Friedens, wie in allen Gemeinen der Heiligen.
Laſſet es alles ehrlich und ordentlich zugehen.
Rom. 15. v. 33
Der GOtt des Friedens ſey mit euch allen! Amen.

Gedruckt im Jahr 1708

"you wicked beggar, get out of this place, this is my hole and you shall not cook here." Then they would seize hold of each other by the hair and strike each other so that frequently the soup, meat and vegetables were spilt upon the ground, and it was evident that an overseer was needed. He took charge of the apartments of the women and put an end to their contentions.

The Straw commissioner gave these poor people fresh straw every two weeks on which to lie down. He was also a coal distributor, since, as it was somewhat rainy about Christmas, the Queen allowed a distribution of coal by the ship load to the poor people, that they might warm themselves.

The last of the camps to break up was the Camberwell which moved to Retriff. A few of them, as in the case of the Redhouse, stopped in Seventh street, and several hundred in St. Stephen. Those who had some provisions, remained here and there in London after their own pleasure, since they could stop comfortably with their own people.

Reaching the place of their entertainment, they were all so treated and accommodated, that no one could with reason complain of anything. Two hundred thousand pounds sterling or five millions, (?) the most gracious Queen Annie gave to us poor people.

Upon reaching the ship which was going to Rotterdam, we were taken in the best manner from England, at the expense of the Queen, with bread, beer, butter, bacon and cheese, and as God himself soon brought us over the sea, the Lord Commissioners were dispatched in the name of the Queen and the whole Parliament to congratulate us. After wishes of good luck had been given, each man received a nine pound loaf of bread, white as snow, and also a Reich gulden in money. We were then ordered to camp in the field and received weekly so much that every man could live respectably. All this they received from the Queen, besides what the princes, counts, barons, merchants and rich citizens daily spent for us. On many days, thirty and even more wagons loaded with bread and cheese were brought into camp, where, there being no purchasers, these

THE
STATE
OF THE
PALATINES
FOR
Fifty YEARS paft
TO THIS
PRESENT TIME.

CONTAINING,

I. An Account of the Principality of the *Palatinate* ; and of the Barbarities and Ravages committed by Order of the *French* King upon the Inhabitants ; Burning to the Ground a great Number of their moft Famous Cities, and throwing the Bones of Emperors, Princes and Prelates, out of their Tombs, &c.

II. The Cafe of the *Palatines.* Publifh'd by themfelves, and Humbly Offered to the Tradefmen of *England*. With a Lift of them, and the Trades which the Men are brought up to.

III. The Humble Petition of the Juftices of *Middlefex* to Her Majefty on their Behalf, with Her Majefties Order thereupon, and an Abftract of the Brief gracioufly Granted for their Subfiftence.

IV. A Letter about Settling and Employing them in other Countries.

V. A Proclamation of the *States-General* for Naturalizing all Strangers, and receiving them into their Country.

VI. Laftly, Their prefent Encamping at *Camberwell* and *Black-heath*, in many Hundred Tents, by Her Majefties Grace and Favour, till they can be otherwife difpos'd of, and how they Employ themfelves ; with their Marriages, Burials, &c. Alfo the great Kindnefs their Anceftors fhew'd to the *Englifh* Proteftants in the Bloody Reign of Queen *Mary*.

(See note 1.)

---

[1] This is another of those rare little booklets called forth during the sojourn of the Palatines in Great Britain. Its aim is fully expressed in the title. It is quite rare, but a few copies being in the libraries of this country. Through the courtesy of the State Library of New York, at Albany, I have been enabled to make myself master of its contents. I hereby desire to make public acknowledgment to the Officers of the said Library for having with the utmost readiness placed the book at my disposal. Only persons engaged in work like this can appreciate such favors properly.

things were freely distributed. Besides this, many rich gentle-men brought 60 or 80 pounds or as many Reichthalers and dis-tributed them among the entire German people, and while doing so, said very modestly, "Take this now, with my Sympathy."

Many thousands of naked, and also such as out of greed locked up their own clothing in their chests, and went about in rags, were clothed anew.

A single business man, a Quaker, had for eight days cut up many wagon loads of cloth, for the naked ones. An-other one bought out nearly all the Shoemakers ; even before, he had bought 32.000 pairs of shoes which he gave to the people. And still another distributed 18,489 shirts so that those who were ill-clad might go better dressed. It would be hard to say how much the court preacher, now an inspector at Magdeburg, John Tribekko, spent in behalf of the Germans.

On the whole, our weak tongues can never tell the excellent deeds of charity which we Germans in England enjoyed. But sighing, we can only pray to God, that he may return it to them a thousand fold.

And likewise, as pure wheat is never entirely without weeds, or seldom a herd which has not one sickly member, so also among these many rich benefactors there were at times wicked outcasts who made it all the more bitter for the Germans. But the trouble came mostly by means of those Catholics who we previously had with us. At one time, while we were still camp-ing in the fields, there came more than 1800 English people, on a dark night, with scythes and other weapons to our camp, who desired to cut down all the Catholics. This, indeed, with-out doubt would have been accomplished had they not been with the Lutherans and Reformed. To this day, on December 4 (1711) the pope is burned in effigy in all the streets of the city of London, and in all England, showing thereby how favorable they must have been to the Catholics!

Among the other dissolute outcasts there was a Presbyterian, born of the devil, a clerical, one devoid of all common sense, who had run away from Switzerland, and was now seeking to make it very bitter for these Germans. He represented them to the Queen and Parliament as wearing blue stockings, and declaring they should be allowed to perish like dogs. As he received but little attention, he placed himself behind the recruiting officers, and as if he had royal authority, took away the finest and youngest boys as soldiers on the men of war and in other military service, and swore like a common foot soldier. He indulged in tobacco, beer and whisky from morning until night, and had, like Sminderides for 20 years, or so long as he had been in England, never seen the sun rise or set, sober. In such a prolonged carousal he pleased all the poor Englishmen. He took away the children from the poor Germans, and played with them as a Jew would do. For when a poor Englishman obtained a child to whom he promised to teach his profession, the Queen gave him five pounds sterling : when they had the money they supported the child very well for a week or two, but after that gave him blows instead of bread, so that because of his extreme hunger he was forced to run away.

Finally, after such religious malice was discovered, it was made known to the public and upon the knowledge of this Pharaoh-like oppression, there began the German emigration from England to other countries and islands, bringing them to dire distress. The beginning of this movement was made by those who went into Ireland, numbering 3688 persons. They were badly accommodated. They had to endure hunger and cold keep several fast days every week, as they had nothing to eat. No one ever received anything he could call his own. He might go wheresoever he would, but he must remain, together with his own people, a slave and a bondsman.

First those in Liverpool followed those who had gone over into Ireland at the breaking up of the camp. Or rather 30 families or 126 persons of those in Liverpool followed after them. They were very excellent people, and artisans but were so well supported by their hard labor, that after they had consumed their own provisions they could drive away hunger. Sixteen families went into Sunderland, 120 miles from London, to a

Prince who promised them so much ground, but did not keep his promise. Instead, he made day laborers of them and at last even went so far as to make those who did not escape in the night, slaves, sending them to Jamaica. Ten families proceeded to the West Country, otherwise called Plymouth, to earn their bread, in the Alaunen mountains. They received plenty of work but little pay. Now an Englishmen in those days received a Reich gulden for his daily wages, but the Germans only got a half Kopfferstücke. Thereupon they all turned their faces towards London, so that they might go back to Germany again.

Two families or fourteen people went to a gentleman 40 miles from London, at a place called Northumberland, who received only one pound of salt weekly among them, and daily they received half a pound of bread. Besides this they received neither meat nor vegetables of any kind. One family numbering eight was taken to a certain gentleman in the country, who promised them golden mountains, but in reality compelled them to herd swine. The head of this family was a hunter and an excellent man of the Reformed religion, and whose name I could give for the information of his friends. But he has escaped with wife and children, and with the others, who perhaps were not allowed to return to the Fatherland, went to New York.

Eight hundred and forty-four poor persons from Switzerland were put on board a ship to sail to North Carolina, but were anchored half a year at Portsmouth in the greatest hunger. 3086 persons were embarked on ten ships to be transported to New York, but they were already on the sea for eighteen weeks, from Christmas to Easter, and will leave port only with the fleet. It was their intention to enter some humble employment and if they could earn enough to buy property, they would become landholders. 1600 persons were packed on two ships to go to the Scilly islands, but when the inhabitants of that place received news of their coming, they sent a woefully worded petition to Parliament stating they could not support themselves much less the Germans, who did not understand fishing and

A BRIEF

HISTORY

OF THE

Poor *Palatine* Refugees,

Lately Arriv'd in

ENGLAND.

Containing,

I. A full Anfwer to all Objections made againft re-
ceiving them ; and plain and convincing Proofs, that
the Acceffion of Foreigners is a manifeft Advantage
to *Great Britain*, and no Detriment to any of her
Majefty's native Subjects.
II. A Relation of their deplorable Condition ; and
how they came to be reduc'd to fuch Extremities.
III. A Defcription of the Country from whence they
came.
IV. An Account of their Numbers.
V. By what Methods they have been fubfifted.
VI. How they may be difpos'd of, to the Honour and
Service of the Queen's Majefty, the Glory and Pro-
fit of this Kingdom, and the Advantage of them-
felves and Pofterities. And
VII. An exact Lift of the Names of the Commiffioners
and Truftees appointed by her Majefty, for receiving
and difpofing of the Money to be collected for the
Subfiftance and Settlement of the faid *Palatines*.

In a LETTER *to a Friend in the Country.*

LONDON Printed : And Sold by *J. Baker* at the *Black Boy*
in *Pater-Nofter-Row*. 1709. Price 6 d.

(See note 2 on page 399.)

could not ward off hunger. After six weeks had passed they were again set on land, and went to Germany again accompanied by their Lutheran pastor.

Three hundred and twenty two young people went into the English military service. The English bought 141 children, boys and girls.   Fifty six young persons were used as servants, besides these there were other families here and there that no one knew of, because they went out of the company without leaving their names. Of these there came back into Germany again, the following :

I. 3548 on the 29th of September, 1708 (1709?) went back to the Fatherland again.

II. 1600 who were to go to the Scilly islands went back again.

III. The 746 who were ordered to go to Ireland, had to go to Germany.

IV. 800 from Ireland came also upon German soil again.

In a like manner all those who escaped from Plymouth, Sunderland, Liverpool, and other places were also sent out of England. In all, these numbered 6994 souls. To Ireland, North Carolina, New York and other places, 8213 were sent. This number must be added to those who had gone into Germany, making a total of 15,201. The whole number that came to England was 32,468, and subtracting from this total the before

---

² This little book of 50 pages is one of the most valuable contributions to the history of my subject, I have found. It came into my hands more than six months after this article had been prepared, and while it contains little that I had not found in detached fragments elsewhere, it is nevertheless one of the fullest, and as I believe one of the most reliable of all the authorities that have survived the mutations of two centuries. The copy I have used is the property of Judge Pennypacker, who received it from his London agent only a few months ago. In my searches through some of the principal libraries of the country, I did not find a copy, and had no knowledge of its existence until its contents were placed at my service by its generous owner. It is possibly unique, and it were well, perhaps, if the Pennsylvania-German Society, should some day publish the little book entire.

mentioned 15,201 there were in all 17,261 who died in London and other parts of England, not taking into account the 200 who went down with the ship and those who were buried at sea and in Holland.

As long as the Germans were encamped, things went tolerably well in spite of the fact that most of the parents permitted their innocent children to become corrupt, and cared not if they died, not even going to their funerals. But there were other good people who buried them. To these funerals many hundred Englishmen went, both on foot and in wagons. Frequently the concourse made such a noise, both by the neighing of the horses, rattling of wheels and by their loud talking, that no one could hear the minister or schoolmaster who officiated.

As those still living were moved into quarters, a hundred or more together, and lodged there, one could then see among other things what these wicked people brought from Germany, who left their own people without counsel, help or comfort, to die like cattle. They did not bury their children decently but permitted them to be dragged along like carcasses. Ordinarily, at 2 o'clock in the afternoon, a signal was given to bury the dead, by means of sheep and cow bells, whereupon the men, two by two brought the corpse of an adult, hanging from a sort of a carrying frame, and these were followed by the corpses of the small and half-grown children, borne upon the heads of women, to the cemetery at Dertforth.[10] Perhaps half a dozen old women accompanied these funeral processions. (Weiber die mit in Engeland Würtz nägelein in Carolin zulesan gekommen.) As soon as the procession reached the cemetery, the corpses were thrown into a hole in layers, like herring. First were laid the women and virgins ; upon these men and young boys, and upon these were placed the children, lengthwise and crosswise, until the hole was full.

---

[10] This practice is pursued in some Spanish American countries at the present day, with the accompaniments of men firing salutes from muskets and others playing on violins.

Frequently it happened that when they carried out the dead and there were no ditches ready, they were put into coffins made of old boards and placed behind the encampment walls, from which they were taken by the dogs and entirely devoured. [—gantzlich aus den Sargen heraus nahmen und von ihnen Speisten.]

Those who were in other quarters, as the Redhouse, and remained with the Lutheran ministers, had it far better, for they were buried in a Christian manner, with beautiful hymns and a funeral panegyric. These services were usually conducted by Master George Hainer and the Schoolmaster, John George Tiltz. Rightly it was said of the Palatines, for so the Germans were commonly called in England, "you hit them, but they do not feel it." For if the evil Spirit choked and killed them, there was nothing but rejoicings and marriages among them. The before mentioned George Hainer himself joined 248 couples, and it is not definitely known how many were married by the others, namely by Master John Tribekko and Mr. Ruperti, before his arrival. 308 children were baptized by Mr. Hainer, five of whom were illegitimate, and thirteen were baptized at sea.

Nor should the remarkable marriage act be passed over in silence, which Mr. Hager accomplished after his ordination. Truly, he who could have seen this marriage ceremony performed as I saw it, would have laughed until his belly shook. In the first place, as Mr. Hager took his position in front of an old barrel full of cobbler's wax, and had mumbled a few words, a bridegroom came up who was lame in his left foot, accompanied by his bride, who was lame in the right foot. Truly they looked like children of Vulcan. Along with these came another couple, a very loving pair. The bride was more than 60 years old and had a hundred thousand wrinkles, in which foxes and hares could have hidden themselves; in other respects she looked much like a stuck calf. The groom was 18 or 19 years old, not yet dry behind the ears. He supported himself at the girdle of the bride, much like a child when it is learning to

Canary-Birds Naturaliz'd

I N

UTOPIA.

A CANTO.

Dulce eſt paternum ſolum.

L O N D O N

Printed : And ſold by the Bookſellers.
Price Six-pence.
(See note 3.)

walk. The third pair, however, looked a little more graceful. The groom on account of sickness, was so weak he could hardly stand. The bride had a large eye and a small one, and was barefooted and ragged. Meanwhile, she would cast furtive glances upon her beautiful "Corydon" like a cat upon a mouse. This most honorable couple wound up the company as they were all gathered around the barrel. The minister spoke a few words and then they were all joined. Whereupon they all went

---

3 While a number of brochures and booklets were written for and in the interests of the Palatines in England, a few were also written from an opposing standpoint, and this is one of them. It is more curious than meritorious. It is however exceedingly rare, the one whose title page is photographed above being the only copy I have ever seen. It belongs to Judge Samuel W. Pennypacker, in whose library great rarities and early Americana are as numerous as second-hand novels at a street bookstall.

The booklet is a protest against the encouragement, naturalization, and establishment of the Palatines in Great Britain, and the argument is presented in the form of a story. The foreign interlopers are called canary birds, and a council of native birds is called to take action in the matter. The robin, the sparrow, the linnet, the lark, nightingale and the rest meet in council and in their most melodious strains show up the bad character of the canaries, and declare themselves opposed to affording them entertainment. But many other birds dissented. The crow, magpie, goose and eagle upheld the cause of the foreign canaries, and the latter triumphed. Of course the existing factions, interests and prominent persons are represented under these allegorical names, but who is intended can only be surmised.

With a few brief extracts, I shall dismiss this rare example of the Palatine literature of the period.

> In our unhappy Days of *Yore*,
> When foreign Birds from *German* Shore
> Came flocking to *Utopia's* Coast
> And o'er the Country, rul'd the Roast.
> We bought 'em dear, and fed 'em well
> 'Till they began for to rebel.
>
> *   *   *   *   *   *
>
> Or shall such Interlopers come
> And turn me out of House and Home?

away from each other, like goats when they go away from their shepherd, each one to his own place.

Now, at last, when everybody was married that could go or stand, their hopes were disappointed because Parliament would not give its consent to what the Queen had promised. Upon this, the preachers were ordered by the committee to make known in sermons and at prayer-meeting, that those who desired to return to the Fatherland, should so decide and give their

---

> Besides they're not of our Religion
> No more than any *Holland* Widgeon.
>
>   *   *   *   *   *   *
>
> Perhaps in Time they'll take, forsooth
> The Bread out of our Natives Mouth,
> To nat'ralize 'em is a Jest
> Lets not defile our own dear Nest.
>
>   *   *   *   *   *   *
>
> And will these Foreigners be found
> To till your waste and barren ground?
> In good Mechanics their Trades follow
> And let your fruitful Fields lie fallow.
> We've Poor enough among ourselves ;
> Need no encroaching foreign Elves.
>
>   *   *   *   *   *   *

Here is a tilt at William Penn :

> At this, a quaking *Bird* o' the Feather
> Native, was highly nettl'd whether
> We'd nat'ral such vast Flocks together;
> Or how we'd of them so dispose
> As not to make intestine Woes ;
> But on the Wing his ruffl'd Pen
> Was quickly set to Rights again,
> And by advancing his Dominion
> Made the best Feather in his 'Pinion.
> For presently the higher Pow'rs
> Prevail'd by plying the next Oars ;
> To stop his mouth they found a way
> And sent them to 'Sylvania.

names, for each one was to receive a pound sterling for the expenses of the journey. Upon this more than 900 people gathered together and returned again to Germany. The rest who remained in England, thought they would stay there, as it was a country in which the earth was so fruitful, that in many respects it could be compared to the promised land. In a word, it was an earthly Paradise. Yet good and excellent as the land was, in spite of it all, the Germans were forced to make room and go again upon German soil. But the most of these people went to Dantzig. How contented they all will be there, experience will tell us.

APPENDIX G.

ANOTHER ACCOUNT OF THE STAY OF THE PALATINES IN AND
AROUND LONDON —DETAILS OF THE MEASURES ADOPTED
TO SUBSIST THEM DURING THEIR STAY AND TO PROVIDE
FOR THEIR PERMANENT SETTLEMENT.[13]

SEAL OF WILLIAM PENN.

ER Majesty being informed of the miserable Condition of these People, was at the whole Charge of transporting them into her own Dominions, and took particular Care of their Subsistence ; but their Numbers being like to increase, and it must necessarily take up some Time for appointing and settling the Distribution of her Majesty's Charity for their daily Relief, a certain Number of well disposed private Gentlemen, Divines, Physicians, Merchants and Characters, whose names I have no authority to publish, and

---

[13] Palatine Refugees in England, p. 30.

whose indefatigable Pains and unexemplify'd Charities, nothing less than Heaven can recompense, voluntarily, and without any Invitation or Motive, but their own pious Inclinations obliging them to it; 1st, Because the Palatines were in great Distress. 2dly, Because they were Strangers; And 3dly, Because it was not known that the Government, or any else provided, for them. In which good Offices they laboured abundantly and effectually, from about the Middle of May, till the 2d of July, at which time Commissioners were appointed by her Majesty's Letters Patent, to take Care of 'em, and receive Proposals for the Disposal of 'em, whereof all these private Gentlemen aforesaid, are of the Number.

In order to make Provision for these distressed People, when these Gentlemen acted in a private Capacity, they first met in a room in the Temple Change Coffee House, and afterwards at a Gentleman's Chambers in the Queen's-Bench Walks, in the Temple, where they erected themselves into a Charitable Society, elected a Chairman, and came to such Resolutions as were thought most expedient for the Subsistence of the Palatines. To which End they chose two Agents to attend these People *de Die in Diem*, to inform themselves and then the Gentlemen, of their Several Conditions, and to distribute the private Charities in such Proportion as they saw convenient, 'till Places might be found to lodge them in, without any trouble to the Inhabitants ; and besides these Particulars, by their Interest with the Nobility, Gentry, Merchants and others, they procur'd as much private Charity from several Hands, during the short Time of their acting as private Gentlemen, as amounted to between 7 and 800 Pounds ; Many of which Benefactors, in Obedience to that Evangelical Precept, of not letting the left Hand know what the right Hand does, in this kind, conceal'd their Names from this Charitable Society ; tho' the Gentlemen never omitted returning their hearty thanks to the Benefactors by the Persons that brought it.

The private Charities thus Collected, these Gentlemen ordered to be put into the Hands of a Goldsmith, which was employ'd for the Subsistence of the Distressed ; and whereas several of them, at their first coming were in great Want, all imaginable Care and Speed was us'd to procure them Lodging by their Agents, the number of whom they encreas'd with the Number of the Palatines, to whom they allow'd and pay'd 12s. per week for their Pains and Subsistence, besides other necessary Charges and Expenses in the Service of the necessitous Palatines.

About this Time, viz. May 23, 1709, there was an estimate produc'd, that the Number of the Palatines were 825 Men, Women and Children, residing about the Tower, St. Cathrenes, Tower Ditch, Wapping, Nightingale Lane, East Smithfield and Places adjacent, whereupon it was agreed by the Gentlemen to thin the Number, by hiring some cheap Houses and Barns out of the Town ; which was done accord-

ingly, and they were lodg'd in Barns and Houses at Kensington, Walworth, Stockwell, Bristoll, Cansey, and Camberwell ; and as the Number of the Palatines encreas'd, so did the Care of these Gentlemen, in providing more Barns and Houses for them; also in procuring from the Queen Lodging for them in her Majesty's Rope Yard at Deptford, in the upper Rooms in the Red House in the same Place, which the Queen hir'd and were then vacant, with the Loan of a thousand Tents from her Majesty, for their Reception on Blackheath, Greenwich and Camberwell, where a Gentleman of that place gave a Ground to set them up in. Nor did the Care of these Gentlemen terminate in Lodging them, but they also suppli'd them with great Quantities of Bread, Cheese, Milk and Small Beer with Straw to lie on, Blankets and Cover-lids and as many Combs as cost £12.

They also took Care when any of the Palatines were sick, to provide Necessaries fit for them in such a Condition, and a

THE PENNSYLVANIA-GERMAN SOCIETY.

learn'd and charitable Physician of their own Number, took the Pains to visit them, and supply'd them with Physical Medicaments at his own Expense, as well as leaving a Chirurgeon behind him, to administer them according to his Direction.

But all these being corporal Charities, these Gentlemen ceas'd not here, but also made Provision for Spirtual Food for their Souls : and to that pious End, agreed with Mr. Sc——r to read Prayers to the Palatines every Day, for which he was to be allow'd the Charge of his Coach-hire; the Clerk of the Prussian chappel was to assist at divine Service, and to be consider'd for his Pains. To farther improve their knowledge in the Word of God, these Gentlemen desir'd one of their Num-

ARMS OF CHUR—BRAUNSCHWEIG.
1694.

ber to write to his correspondent at Hamburg, to buy and send over a thousand High Dutch New Testaments, and the Psalms in Prose, in Quires in the Long Primer, for the Use of the Palatines, and order'd that £60 should be reserv'd to pay for them. Lastly, they agreed that it should be taken into Consideration, how to form a Proposal to the Government, for applying the Queen's Allowance to support five hundred Palatine Children, from the Age of six to twelve, at a Charity School, in order to be instructed to write and read English, to be taught their Catechism, to cast Accompt, and to work on the Linnen Manufactures, &c. And now these private Gentlemen having voluntarily done all these great and charitable Offices for the Palatines, they put an End to their Meeting in the Temple, and the Trustees appointed by her Majesty to distribute the Money collected for the Palatines, met the first Time, viz. July 2d at the New Building joining the Banquetting House, and adjourn'd themselves to the next Wednesday Morning at St. Paul's Chaple House. * * * * *

The Queen's great Charity has, ever since the first Arrival of the Palatines, been the principal Fund for their Subsistence, the other Charities, though they did abundance of Good, as an additional Relief, by the prudent Management of the Gentlemen, yet they were but precarious, and not to be rely'd upon; so that her Majesty's Charge, by the Increase of these Foreigners, was raised from £16 a Day, at first, to £100 a Day afterwards ; which was distributed by the two German Divines (that only had Authority to dispose of it) in this Proportion, viz. To each Man, and each Woman above twenty Years of Age five Pence. To those under twenty, and above ten, four Pence. To those under ten Years of Age, three Pence *per diem*, which was pay'd every Tuesday and Friday, besides one Pound of Bread *per diem* to each of 'em : but there being only two Gentlemen, as has already been said, that had Authority to receive and dispose of the Queen's Charity, to whom it grew a greater Burden then they were able to bear, it was thought convenient by the Ministry, to put the care of the Palatines under a due Regulation, by authorizing a Number of Persons, fitly qualify'd, to enquire into their State, and the properest Measure for their Relief and Settlement ; whereupon her Majesty was graciously pleased to appoint Commissioners and Trustees ; by her Letters Patents under the Great Seal, for Collecting, receiving, and disposing of the Money to be collected for the Subsistence and Settlement of the poor Palatines, who upon July 6, 1709, gave publick Notice in the *Gazette*, that they would meet in a general Meeting in the Chapter House of St. Pauls, on every Wednesday at four of the Clock in the afternoon, and that in order to receive Proposals for employing and settling the said Palatines, and to prepare Business for the said general Meeting, they would meet as a Committee in the new Buildings adjoining to the Banquetting House in Whitehall, on every Tuesday, Thursday, and Saturday, at four of the Clock in the afternoon ; and that they would also meet as a Committee in the Council Chamber in Guild-hall, London, on every Monday and Friday at four of the clock in the Afternoon, and on every Wednesday at ten of the Clock in the Morning, the first of the said Meetings to be on the Friday following.

APPENDIX H.

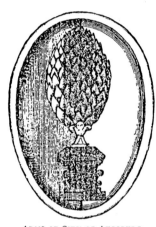

JN the rare book belonging to Judge Pennypacker of which I have already spoken,[10] I found the following summary of the persons who left Germany during this Exodus, as well as the places from which they emigrated. How the writer who prepared it was able to get at the exact numbers it is difficult to say at this distant day, and yet, it is possible his figures may be approximately correct. It will be observed the sum total does not reach the half of that of the writer quoted in Appendix F.

F. R. D.

LISTE DER NACH DER INSEL PENSYLVANIEN ABGEREISTEN LEUTE.

Aus der Pfaltz 8,589
Aus dem Darmstattichen 2,334

[10] Das verlangte, nicht erlangte Canaan.

Aus dem Hanauischen	1,113
Aus dem Francken-Land[1]	653
Aus dem Mahntzischen[2]	63
Aus dem Trierischen[3]	58
Aus dem Speyrischen, Wormsischen und Graff-schafftlichen[4]	490
Aus dem Hessenland[5]	81
Aus dem Zweybrückischen[6]	125
Aus dem Nassauischen[7]	203
Aus dem Elsass	413
Aus dem Baadischen[8]	320
Aus allerhand Landschaften ledige Hand-wercks Leute	871
Summa	15,313

ANOTHER SUMMARY, TO JUNE 10, 1709.[11]

By June 10, there had come over the following:

Men that had families	940
Unmarried men	292
Daughters above fourteen years of age	247
Sons under fourteen years	1016
Wives	903
Widows	73
Unmarried women	77
Sons above fourteen years	257
Daughters under fourteen years	950
A Total of	4,774

[1] Land of the Franks. Now belonging to Bavaria, called Kreise or counties; Ober, Mittel and Unter Franken, including the cities of Nuremberg, Baireuth and Würzburg.

[2] The Archbishopric of Mayence (Mainz).

[3] The Archbishopric of Trier.

4 The Ecclesiastical districts of Speir, Worms and Grafschaftlich of the Palatinate Rhine Provinces.

5 From Hesse Darmstadt (Electorate.)

6 From the district of Zweibrücken, a city of the Palatinate.

7 From Hesse-Nassau (Cassel) Electorate.

8 From Baden.

11 State of the Palatines, p. 7.

UTROQUE PARATUS.

2. The German Emigration to America

By

Henry Eyster Jacobs

This chapter is a facsimile of material which appeared as: Henry Eyster Jacobs, "The German Emigration to America," *Pennsylvania German Society Proceedings and Addresses* 8(1898).

Contents

1. The Effort to Turn German Emigration to South
   Carolina   31

2. The Immediate Results of Kocherthal's Pamphlet
                                                    44

3. The Palatine Emigration to New York   63

4. On the Ocean   80

5. In New York   110

6. To Pennsylvania   134

PREFATORY NOTE.

The great movement of thousands of Palatines, accompanied by some Swabians and other Germans to England in the spring and summer of 1709, was traced in a most exhaustive and satisfactory manner last year. They had been preceded, it will be remembered, by a small band under the Rev. Joshua Kocherthal, who, after some delay in England, had reached New York on the last day of 1709. It is our aim to take up the narrative at this point, and, after following the course of the immigrants to Pennsylvania, to give some account of succeeding emigrations, until the year 1740.

CHAPTER I.—THE EFFORT TO TURN GERMAN EMIGRATION TO SOUTH CAROLINA.

KOCHERTHAL, upon whose tombstone at West Camp, New York, may still be read the inscription that he was "the Joshua to the High Germans in America,"[1] had been pastor at Landau, the now flourishing town in Bavaria, that had suffered exceedingly from repeated invasions by the French. In the year 1704, after the invasion of 1703, he had .visited England to inquire into the expediency of an emigration of his people to America. The information which he gathered he embodied in a brochure, the first edition of which was pub-

[1] " Wisse Wandersman | Unter diesem Steine ruht | nebst seiner Sibylla Charlotte | Ein rechter Wandersmann | Der Hoch-Teutschen in America | ihr Josua | Und derselben an Der ost und west seite | Der Hudson Rivier | rein lutherischer Prediger | Seine erste ankunft war mit L'd Lovelace | 1707 / 8 den 1. Januar | Seine sweite mit Col. Hunter | 1710 d. 14 Juny | Seine Englandische reise unterbrach | Seine Seelen Himmlische reise | an St. Johannis Tage 1719 | Begherstu mehr zu wissen | So unter Suche in Welanchthons vaterland | Wer war dex de Kocherthal | Wer Harschias | Wer Winchenbach | B. Berkenmayer S. Heurtein L Brevort | MDCCXLII."

Außführlich
und
Umständlicher Bericht ·
Von der berühmten Landschafft

CAROLINA,

In dem
Engelländischen America
gelegen.

An Tag gegeben
Von

Kocherthalern.

Zweyter Druck.

Franckfurt am Mäyn/
Zu finden bey Georg Heinrich Oehrling/
Anno 1709.

Pamphlet circulated by Kocherthal advising emigrants to go to Carolina.

lished in 1706, and the second edition at Frankfort on the Main in 1709. The title of this little volume, intended to advocate the claims of South Carolina in preference to those of Pennsylvania as the goal of German Emigration is: "Full and Circumstantial Report concerning the Renowned District of Carolina in English America."

Under what influence he had reached his conclusions he does not state. But the comparatively weak stream of immigrants that flowed to Pennsylvania in the first decade of the Eighteenth Century, in response to the many appeals, indicates a dissatisfaction and distrust, that suggested inquiries into the availability of other parts of America for German colonists. His argument in favor of choosing Carolina for the settlement, was preceded by ten chapters, concerning the land in general, the government, the fertility of the soil, the climate, the security, the voyage, etc. While the ordinary assignment of land was fifty acres to every head of a family, Mr. Kocherthal states that he has been promised one hundred and fifty, or even two hundred acres to each, in case the number of immigrants be large. The terms provide that the land shall be free for the first three years, and that, afterwards, the nominal rent shall be a penny per acre annually. With its glowing description of the fertility of the soil in wheat, rye, oats, barley and Indian corn, and its adaptation to the cultivation of the vine and tobacco, of olives and cotton; with the opportunities portrayed for the manufacture of silk by its facilities for the raising of mulberry trees; with an account of forests, full of valuable timber, and the

vision of mines, rich in iron and lead; with a remarkable
statement concerning the salubrity of the climate, where
the temperature of the winter was no more rigorous than
April or October in the Palatinate, and the summer, while
warmer, was tempered by almost constant cool breezes,
where the days were two hours shorter in summer, and
two hours longer in winter than in Germany; and with
assurances of the friendship of the Indians, and the freedom offered by the Government, we can readily understand how the book spread among oppressed and impoverished people dissatisfaction with their homes, and enkindled
the desire to cross the ocean to the new land of promise.

Pennsylvania, it was conceded, had certain advantages.
German settlements had already been founded, and the
fruits of the soil were chiefly those to which Germans were
accustomed. But these, it was maintained, were overbal-
anced by the eternal summer, and never failing pasturage,
and less expensive homes and clothing for colonists, and
shelter for the wintering of cattle. The voyage to Pennsylvania required an immediate outlay, while all the expense of the trip to Carolina could be defrayed by subsequent service in the colony.

To the credit of Kocherthal, be it said that he did not
hide any of the dangers and difficulties in the way of removal to America. The peril of the long sea voyage and
the many hardships to be faced after landing were faith-
fully narrated. His readers were warned against being
influenced by the desire for riches, or for an easy life, or
by the love of adventure, and mere curiosity. The oppor-

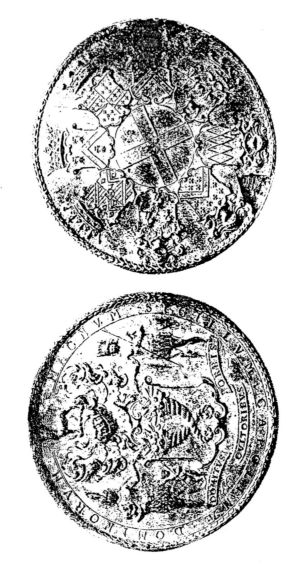

THE PENNSYLVANIA-GERMAN SOCIETY.

COPY OF A WAX IMPRESSION OF THE "GREAT SEAL OF THE LORDS PROPRIETORS OF THE PROVINCE OF CAROLINA," SHOWING UPON THE REVERSE THE ARMS OF THE EIGHT LORDS PROPRIETORS.

ORIGINAL IN PUBLIC RECORDS OFFICE, LONDON.

tunity was one only for those, for whom all other support
had failed. His closing statement, that, in the year 1708,
or at farthest, in the spring of 1709, he intended to set out
for Carolina, with his family and a number of others, and
his invitation, upon certain conditions, for additional recruits, carry us to the very source of the Palatinate movement to England as the portal to America.

So inaccessible is this volume to most investigators, that
an extended synopsis is here given:

"CHAPTER I.—*Of the Country.*

"Boundaries of Carolina. Division into North and
South Carolina. Advantages of the latter: Settled
along the Ashley and Cooper rivers, with some Re-
formed Swiss along the Santee. Otherwise South
Carolina is unsettled. Distance from nearest part of
South Carolina to nearest part of Pennsylvania, 100
German miles. Route: From Germany to Holland;
thence to England; thence southwest to 900 or 1000
German miles. Coast low; interior elevated, with
some high mountains.

"CHAPTER II.—*Of the Government.*

"South Carolina was given by the King of England in 1663 to some noblemen, as a reward for fidelity,
who have transmitted it by inheritance to present
owners. Government consists of eight persons, of
whom Lord Granville is President. A governor rules
in their name. Religious freedom assured Reformed
and Lutherans alike, and also to the Mennonites.
Every head of a family can procure 50 acres, or, if
he need them, 100 acres of land. As a special favor,

150 or even 200 acres were offered Kocherthal, in case a large number settle together. Any unsettled portion of Province may be chosen by settlers under this offer. No rent for first three years ; afterwards, a penny an acre annually ; but as another special favor, if a large number of settlers accompany him, the number of free years will be extended, possibly as high as seven. Tithes will be required for Church purposes. Removal to another province permissible at any time, upon payment of all debts, and due notice to the Government. Mechanics will be required to pay only a few pence of taxes annually. Hunting and fishing free, the only restriction being that of not trespassing on lands of other settlers, or coming too close to the Indians.

"Chapter III.—*Of the Fruitfulness of the Soil.*

" South Carolina is one of the most fruitful countries to be found. Far surpasses England and Germany. But districts vary in their productivity. Two crops of Indian corn may be raised in a season. No better rice is raised in any land. It is an extensive article of commerce. French settlers have been very successful in the cultivation of grapes. Tobacco rivals that of Virginia. Apples, pears, plums, quinces, etc., may be raised from seed, which settlers should bring with them. The mulberry tree offers opportunities for silk-culture. Much may be expected from the raising of cotton. Olives, citrons, figs, pomegranates flourish. Although iron and lead mines have been opened, yet as it requires a large amount of capital to work them, settlers should bring their iron tools with them. All sorts of domestic animals may be raised. Cattle need not be housed in winter, which in South Carolina has the temperature of April or October in Germany. Swine may be raised with scarcely any cost, since the forests abound in acorns. Rare opportunities for hunting, especially of swans, ducks, geese and other water fowls. A cow may be bought for an English pound. The cultivation of indigo and tea offers rich returns.

"CHAPTER IV.—*Of the Climate.*

" Occasionally, some snow or ice, early in the morning during winter, but it disappears by eight or nine o'clock. While the heat in summer is considerably greater than in Germany, yet at sunset a cool breeze tempers the atmosphere, and renders it more tolerable than in Virginia, notwithstanding the fact that the latter is farther north. The weather not uniform. Places and seasons differ. Generally the climate is very healthful. The Indians used frequently to attain the age of 100, but their age limit has been shortened, since they have learned from Europeans to be intemperate in eating and drinking. It requires some months for immigrants to be acclimated. Carolina unsurpassed in abundance of medicinal herbs.

"CHAPTER V.—*Of Peace and Security.*

" Not only entire peace, but, so far as man can foresee, no future wars, ever to be apprehended. The Indians all friendly, and, besides, ignorant of European modes of warfare. On the right, the other English settlements form a barrier and protection against all possible attacks, while, on the left, the Spaniards are so few, that they fear the English, rather

than the latter them. Sand bars exclude enemies by
sea. The scene of the naval war which England is
carrying on with the French and Spaniards, is on the
Caribbean Sea, 100 to 150 German miles from Carolina. Although there are some wolves in wild portions of the Province, they prey upon other animals
that abound, and rarely attack men. Serpents are
not more numerous than in Italy, Spain and other
warm countries, and avoid the settlements.

"CHAPTER VI.—*Of Commerce.*

"Carolina has an extraordinary number of navi-
gable rivers, rendering the transport of the fruits of
the soil from the interior to other parts of the Province,
the West Indies and Europe, most easy. Coins, with
some slight difference, the same as with us. Final
decision in all matters of litigation made according to
English law and custom.

"CHAPTER VII.—*Of European Nations already
in Carolina: Cities and Towns.*

"Thirty years since Carolina was first settled by
English people. Three nationalities now represented,
viz.: the English, the Dutch and the French. No
Germans as yet, but most of the Dutch not only can
understand, but even speak the German. Charleston,
founded in 1680, on the Ashley and Cooper, and New
London, on the Edisto, are chief places, and must
be regarded as towns, rather than cities. All sorts
of wares may be purchased in Charleston, yet, as
the proportion of mechanics to the population is not
as great as among us, prices are higher. Immigrants
should bring with them as many implements as pos

sible, especially those which are necessary for building. There are a number of schools. In Charleston, there is a Latin School, and in Virginia, a High School. The English, besides endeavoring to Christianize the Indians, are attempting to diffuse a literature among them.

" CHAPTER VIII.—*Of the Disadvantages of the Country.*

" The first and chief want of the country, is people, as the most of the land is unsettled and unpopulated. The length, expense and perils of the voyage. To Germans, it is a great disadvantage that none of their countrymen are there. All other objections are of small account, such as that in the beginning every thing is strange—the greater heat in summer, and the wolves and serpents, of which we have previously made mention.

" CHAPTER IX.—*Of the Voyage from England to Carolina.*

" In time of peace, ships go to Carolina or Virginia, almost every month, but in time of war, generally only in the spring and fall. Spring, the best time. If the wind be constantly favorable, and the voyage in other respects, prosperous, it may be completed in six or even five weeks, in rare cases, even in four; but otherwise it may consume a half a year. In peace, the fare is from five to six pounds sterling; but the cost of a convoy and other expenses, raise it to from seven to eight pounds for every adult. Special arrangements have to be made with the Captain for each half grown child. Persons too poor to pay

RICHARDI BLOME
Englisches
AMERICA,
oder

Kurtze doch deutliche

Beschreibung aller derer
jenigen Länder und Inseln
so der Cron Engeland in West-In-
dien ietziger Zeit zuständig und
unterthänig sind.

durch eine hochberühmte Feder
aus dem Englischen übersetzt
und mit Kupffern gezieret.

❊(o)❊

Leipzig /
Bey Johann Großens Wittbe und Erben.
Anno. 1 6 9 7.

Blome's Description of the English possessions in the Western Hemi-
sphere.

sometimes find proprietors willing to advance the funds, in return for which they serve the latter for some time in Carolina. The period of service, in time of peace, is from two to three years, but when the fare is higher, the time is necessarily longer. Those contemplating such payment, should write to England, and so arrange before starting. The author has endeavored in every way, to secure some other mode of providing for the passage. He has determined, in case a sufficient number to justify the attempt be enrolled, to apply to the Queen to transport them in the hope that they may be carried also on their way from Holland. He is unwilling to ask the favor unless a large number should respond to his proposition. How, in the midst of the other great expenses, and especially those of war, the Queen would be able to assume the responsibility the author does not know. He can make no promises; but can only hope that Divine Providence may open the way. Perils from storms, and, even with the convoy, of pirates must be faced; but ships thus guarded, have for some years been very rarely attacked.

"CHAPTER X.—*Of the Authority for what has been Mentioned.*

"A full report made by a French merchant, du Pre, to a friend in Amsterdam, under date of Maplica, February 17, 1703. Two trustworthy merchants in Holland, by the name of Bujotte, who lived long in Carolina, gave a circumstantial account of the land, in the presence of several other persons. A similar account was received from another London merchant. A number of statements from a sea captain, by the name of Cock. A merchant, by the name of Johnson, gave me a circumstantial account of the country. A clergyman gave much information he had received from the country itself. The Secretary of the Carolina Government also gave an account in the presence of the above mentioned clergyman. A German merchant resident in London, told me of what he had incidentally learned of the country in different places. Almost all the above information was given by the informants separately and independently. Information was also received from the Government. The literature utilized was a little book called Blome's *English America,* translated into the German, and published in Leipzig, 1697, the *Frankfort Relations* 1690, 1700, 1701, various letters in English newspapers concerning Carolina, the *Psychosophia* of Dr. Becher, in which he has written on the colonizing of the West Indies.

" APPENDIX.—*Of Pennsylvania.*

" After referring to Pastorius' *Pennsylvania* and Falckner's *Continuation of the Description of Pennsylvania,* both published at Nuremberg by Otto, Kocherthal, states that in his journey he had met a number of persons who had lived for years in Pennsylvania, and that, therefore, he would give some facts not published in the books mentioned. While Carolina has eternal summer, Pennsylvania has a very severe winter, and one that is not surpassed even in Germany. While in Carolina, the cattle can be kept in the fields all winter, in Pennsylvania they must be housed in barns. Grapes do not flourish as well in Pennsylvania as in Carolina, although the most diligent attempts have been made to cultivate them. In Carolina, people will not suffer in the beginning even in very insignificant huts, whereas the cold winter compels buildings of a very substantial character to be immediately erected for cattle as well as men. The relative expense of clothing must also be remembered. The most desirable lands in Pennsylvania have already been taken. necessitating the purchase of ground from the first occupants, or the payment of much greater ground rent. An immigrant to Pennsylvania must have the money ready with which to prepay his passage, while for one going to Carolina, this is not necessary. Pennsylvania, however, has some advantages : It has German settlers who will aid their countrymen. Its fruits and grains more nearly correspond to those of Germany."

When, then, to this we add the record of lands donated to the Palatines by Queen Anne, along the Broad and Saluda, Congaree and Wateree rivers in South Carolina, near and around the present site of Columbia, the chain of evidence is completed. Although this district, a portion of which is still popularly known to the neighborhood, as "Dutch Fork," was settled by immigrants from southwestern Germany, they represent a late emigration. Some unknown cause intervened to thwart Kocherthal's plans.

CHAPTER II.—THE IMMEDIATE RESULTS OF KOCHERTHAL'S PAMPHLET.

REACHING England in the spring of 1708, Kocherthal's petition to the "Board of Trade" does not mention Carolina, but requests simply "to be sent to one of the plantations,[1] and even this secured a hearing only when three of the Lutheran clergymen of London appeared with him before the Board and pleaded his cause."

The part taken by the pastors of the three Lutheran churches in London deserves especial recognition. The most influential was Anton Wilhelm Boehme, pastor of the German Court Chapel of St. James, born 1643, a native of

---

[1] *Minutes of the Board of Trade*, April 26, 1708. "Mr. Joshua de Kocherthal with three Lutheran ministers (settled here) attending in relation to the ref. from Mr. Scy. Boyle, touching the settlement of the said K. and others in some of Her Majesty's Plantations in America."

Pſalmodia Germanica :

OR, THE

GERMAN PSALMODY,

Tranſlated from the

HIGH DUTCH.

TOGETHER

With their proper TUNES, and thorough BASS.

The THIRD EDITION,
Corrected and very much Enlarged.

*Non Vox, ſed Votum, non Muſica chordula ſed
Cor; non clamans, ſed amans cantat in Aure
Dei.*

LONDON, Printed :

NEW-YORK, Re-printed, and ſold by
H. GAINE, at the *Bible & Crown,* in
Queen-Street, 1756.

Facsimile of title page of *Psalmodia Germanica* (Third Edition); first edition, 1722. (Used by Muhlenberg in English services.)

Pyrmont, an alumnus of Halle, a pupil and frequent correspondent of Francke, and a man of devout spirit and distinguished literary gifts, whose influence was not only very great with Prince George of Denmark, the Queen's husband, whose spiritual adviser he was, but with the Queen herself. Boehme was the most important link between the German churches and the Church of England. It was by his intervention that the "Society for the Propagation of the Gospel in Foreign Parts" adopted and supported the Lutheran missions in East India, after the country passed from the Danish to the English government. His pen was active in the translation of Arndt's *True Christianity* and other standard German works, as well as the Reports of the Halle Mission House, into English, and in the publication in Germany of at least one important book concerning the English Church. Through his intercession Queen Anne endowed a "Free Table" in the Orphan House at Halle.

In the very serious project for a union between the Church of England and the Protestant Church of Germany, that was then the subject of negotiation, with the powerful support of the Queen, and that ceased only with her death, Boehme was probably one of the most important factors. From the arrival of the first emigrants in England, and through all their trials in America, until his death in 1722, they always had in him "a friend at court."[1] Associated with Boehme were George Andrew

---

[1] For biographical sketches of BOEHME, see JOCHER's *Gelehrten Lexicon;* STEPHEN's *Dictionary of National Biography;* Walch's *His-*

Ruperti and John Trebecco, both of whom frequently appeared before the Board of Trade on their behalf. Another official of St. James' Chapel who befriended them was John Christian Jacobi,[1] well-known as the translator of hymns still sung, of which "Holy Ghost Dispel our Sadness" may be cited as an example, and the editor of the *Psalmodia Germanica*, who was occasionally called in to act as interpreter.

After Pastor Kocherthal, with his band numbering originally twenty-six Calvinists and fifteen Lutherans[2]—increased afterwards by a few arrivals from England—had been entrusted to the care of Lord Lovelace, as Governor, and been sent, with generous provision, to New York, the influence of Kocherthal's pamphlet and example continued to work. When the "German Exodus to England" oc-

torische und Theologische Einleitung in die Religion—Streitigkeiten der Ev. Luth. Kirchen, Jena, 1733, Vol. V., pp. 111-399. Burckhardt's *Kirchen-Geschichte der Deutschen Gemeinden in London*, Tübingen, 1798, pp. 77-399. An interesting anecdote illustrating his character is told by Burckhardt, a later London Lutheran pastor. Boehme preached once with such earnestness against adultery that a nobleman in his audience interpreted the sermon as a personal attack, and challenged Boehme to a duel. The challenge was accepted. The pastor appeared on the field in his clerical robe, and with a Bible, instead of a pistol, in his hand. "I regret," he said, "that you were offended at my sermon against a most grievous sin. I can assure you that you were not in my mind. But here I am, armed with the sword of the Spirit, and if your conscience condemns you, I beseech you, for your salvation, to repent and reform your life. If you want to fire I am ready to lay down my life, if your soul only may be saved." List of his numerous publications in *Sammlung auser lesener Materien*, etc. Leipzig, 1733, pp. 38-47.

[1] Mr. Jacobi was Kocherthal's interpreter, Board of Trade Journals, June 14, 1708.

[2] Board of Trade, April 26, 17c8.

Das verlangte / nicht erlangte Canaan bey den Lust-Gräbern;

Oder

Ausführliche Beschreibung

Von der unglücklichen Reise derer jüngsthin aus Teutschland nach dem Engelländischen in America gelegenen

Carolina und Pensylvanien

wallenden Pilgrim / absonderlich dem einseitigen übelgegründeten

Kochenthalerischen Bericht

wohlbedächtig entgegen gesetzt

In

I. Einem Beantwortungs-Schreiben etlicher diese Sach angehenden Fragen; nebst einer Vorrede Moritz Wilhelm Höens.
II. Ermahnungs-Schreiben an die bereits dahin verreißte Teutsche / Anthon Wilhelm Böhmens.
III. Der Berg-Predigt Christi / und Gebettern vor die noch dahin auf dem Weg begriffenen ꝛc.
IV. Königl. Englischen deswegen nach Teutschl. erlassenen Abmahnung.
V. Kurtzen Relation, jener dabey erlittenen Elend und Schicksals.
VI. Noch einer andern Relation davon.
VII. Einem Stück der Warnungs-Predigt t Hn. Johann Tribecks ꝛc. den zuruckreisen in London gehalten.

Alles aus Liebe zur Wahrheit und patriotischem Wohlmeinen zusammen verfasset.

Franckfurt und Leipzig / M DCC XI.

Title page of Rev. Anton Wilhelm Boehme's answer to Kocherthal's "Carolina."

curred Mr. Boehme was not in that country, but the year after he writes that "14,000 persons had gone to England with the expectation of being transported to Carolina." Although Boehme's answer to Kocherthal's pamphlet did not appear until 1711, and is intended to discourage future movements, yet it throws much light upon the details of the emigration to New York.

The book really consists of a series of tracts, the titles of which all appear on its title-page, as follows: "The Canaan, sought for, but not found, by those who till the air; or a full description of the unhappy voyage of the Pilgrims who recently went from Germany to the English possessions in Carolina and Pennsylvania; especially directed against the one-sided, and unfounded report of Kocherthal. I. An Answer to Some Questions on this Subject, with an introduction by Moritz Wilhelm Hoen. II. Admonition to the Germans who have already journeyed thither, by Anton Wilhelm Boehme. III. The Sermon on the Mount, and Prayers, to be used by them, on the way. IV. Dissuasion Against Forsaking Germany by the English Crown. V. Short Account of their Misfortunes. VI. Another Account. VII. An Extract from the Sermon of John Trebecco, delivered in London to the emigrants. All bound together out of love for truth, and patriotic motives. Frankfort and Leipzig, 1711." Each of these parts is paged separately, showing that they were independent publications that were afterwards collected and bound under the one title.

The introduction, written in a Christian spirit, by Moritz Wilhelm Hoen, warns earnestly against the fever for emigration to America, and declares that neither in Europe, nor in America does a Christian have an abiding place. Every one embarking for America must be prepared for troubles, must be ready to die, must have at least one hundred Frankfort florins, and must support his family out of his own purse, for an entire year after his arrival. Penn-

sylvania or Carolina is the question that is then discussed.
The advantages and disadvantages of each are carefully
balanced against one another. The freedom in both provinces is shown to be equal. The excessive heat of South
Carolina renders the raising of European corn difficult,
but adapts it for grape culture. Pennsylvania, Boehme
concludes, is better for the Lower Saxons, who are farmers, while Carolina has advantages for the Palatines and
others, who are wine producers. The argument for emigration, urged from religious motives, claims consideration, and is answered by the sententious remarks : " Some
tell us that they are seeking religious repose. To such
I say, ' The sun that shines at Cologne, shines also at
Paris.' Calm must be sought inwardly, not outwardly.
Every new mode of life has its peculiar temptations." To
those who advised emigration because they believed that
God's judgments upon a sinful land were about to descend,
and that a Zoar or a Pella must be sought for in America,
the sober answer is made, that no Christian has the right
to flee from the judgments that his own sins, as well as
those of others, have called down ; and that if God place
us in the midst of corrupt times, it is our duty not to abandon our post, but to remain, and give our testimony and
make our protest. To the excuse that Germany was per-
vaded by sectarianism, Boehme answers that Pennsylvania has far more sects than Germany. It is, " a *colluvies*
or *Mischmass* of sects, parties and opinions."

Although Pastor Kocherthal never saw the Carolina,
which he had portrayed as a land of milk and honey, some

of those who followed him the next year to England did. The Swiss baron, Christopher de Graffenried and Franz Louis Michel from Berne, reached England that season, with a colony of their countrymen, destined for the district between the Cape Fear and Neuse rivers in North Carolina. They were strengthened by a reinforcement of six hundred and fifty Palatines in two vessels. Most liberal provision was made for giving them an excellent start in their new home. Each family was allowed two hundred and fifty acres of land, without remuneration for five years ; and afterwards upon a rental of two pence per acre, while, upon similar easy terms, they were supplied with agricultural implements, buildings, cattle, clothing and other necessaries. The full text of Graffenried's agreement is as follows :

DE GRAFFENDRIED'S CONTRACT.[1]

"Articles of Agreement, indented and made, published and agreed upon, this tenth day of October, Anno Domino one thousand seven hundred and nine, and in the eighth year of the reign of our sovereign, lady Anne, by the grace of God queen of Great Britain, France and Ireland, defender of the faith, between Christopher de Graffenrid of London esquire and Lewis Mitchell of the same place, of the one part, and sir John Philips bart. sir Alexander Cairnes bart. sir Theodore Janson knt. White Kennet D.D. and dean of Peterborough, John Chamberlain esquire, Frederick Slore doctor of physic, and Mr. Micajah Perry merchant, seven of the commissioners and trus-

---

[1] Williamson's History of North Carolina, I., 275-281.

tees nominated and appointed by her majesty's late gracious letters patent, under the great seal of Great Britain, for the collecting, receiving, and disposing of the money to be collected for the subsistence and settlement of the poor Palatines lately arrived in Great Britain, on the other part.

" Whereas the above named Christopher de Graffenrid and Lewis Mitchell have purchased to themselves and their heirs in fee, and are entitled to a large . tract of land in that part of her majesty's dominions in America called North Carolina, which now lies waste and uncultivated for want of inhabitants; and they the said Christopher de Graffenrid and Lewis Mitchell have applied themselves to the commissioners appointed by the letters patent above mentioned for the subsistence and settlement of the poor depressed Palatines, that some number of the said poor Palatines may be disposed of and settled in the said tract in North Carolina aforesaid, as well for the benefit of the said Christopher de Graffenrid and Lewis Mitchell as for the relief and support of the poor Palatines.

"And whereas the said commissioners have thought fit to dispose of for this purpose six hundred persons of the said Palatines, which may be ninety-two families more or less, and have laid out and disposed of to each of the said six hundred poor Palatines the sum of twenty shillings in clothes, and have likewise paid and secured to be paid to the said Christopher de Graffenrid and Lewis Mitchell the sum of five pounds ten shillings lawful money of Great Britain for each of the said six hundred persons, in consideration of and for their transportation into North Carolina aforesaid, and for their comfortable settlement there.

"It is constituted, concluded and agreed, by and with the said parties to those psents in manner following :

"Inprimis that the said Christopher de Graffenrid and Lewis Mitchell, for the consideration aforesaid, at their own proper costs and charges, shall within the year next after the date hereof, embark or cause to be embarked on ships board, in and upon two several ships, six hundred of such of the said poor Palatines as shall be directed by the said commissioners, which together may in all make up ninety-two families more or less, and cause the said persons to be directly transported to North Carolina aforesaid, providing them with food and other necessaries during their voyage thither.

"Item, that upon the arrival of the said six hundred poor Palatines in North Carolina aforesaid, the said Christopher de Graffenrid and Lewis Mitchell shall, within three months next after their arrival there, survey and set out or cause to be surveyed and set out, by metes and bounds, so much of the said tract of land above mentioned as shall amount to two hundred and fifty acres for each family of the said six hundred poor Palatines, be they ninety-two families, more or less ; and that the said several two hundred and fifty acres for each family be as contiguous as may be for the mutual love and assistance of the said poor Palatines one to another, as well with respect to their exercise of their religion as the management of their temporal affairs.

"And for avoiding disputes and contentions among the said Palatines in the division of the said several two hundred and fifty acres of land, it is agreed that the said land, when so set by two hundred and fifty acres to a family, be divided to each family by lot.

"Item, that the said Christopher de Graffenrid and Lewis Mitchell, their heirs, executors and administrators, within three months rest after the arrival of the said poor Palatines in North Carolina aforesaid, shall give and dispose of unto the said poor Palatines, and to each family by lot, two hundred and fifty acres of the tract of land above mentioned, and by good assurances in law grant and convey the said several two hundred and fifty acres to the first and chief person or persons of each family, their heirs and assigns forever, to be held the first five years thereafter, without any acknowledgment for the same, and rendering and paying unto the said Christopher de Graffenrid and Lewis Mitchell, their heirs, executors and administrators, for every acre the sum of two pence, lawful money of that country yearly and every year after the said term of five years.

"Item, that for and during one whole year after the arrival of the said poor Palatines in North Carolina aforesaid, the said Christopher de Graffenrid and Lewis Mitchell shall provide or cause to be provided for, and deliver to the said poor Palatines sufficient quantities of grain and provision and other things for the comfortable support of life; but it is agreed, that the said poor Palatines respectively repay and satisfy the said Christopher de Graffenrid and Lewis Mitchell, their heirs, executors and administrators, for the full value of what they shall respectively receive on the amount at the end of the first year then next after.

"Item, that the said Christopher de Graffenrid and Lewis Mitchell, at their own proper costs and charges,

within four months after their arrival there, shall provide for the said Palatines and give and deliver or
cause to be given and delivered to them, for their use
and improvement, two cows and two calves, five sows
with their several young, two ewe sheep and two lambs,
with a male of each kind, who may be able to propa-
gate; that at the expiration of seven years thereafter each family shall return to the said Christopher de Graffenrid and Lewis Mitchell, their heirs or
executors, the value of the said cattle so delivered
to them, with a moiety of the stock then remaining in
their hands, at the expiration of the said seven years.

"Item, that immediately after the division of the
said two hundred and fifty acres among the families
of the said Palatines, the said Christopher de Graffenrid and Lewis Mitchell shall give and dispose of
gratis to each of the said Palatines a sufficient number of tools and implements for felling of wood and
building of houses, etc.

"And lastly, it is covenanted, constituted and
agreed, by and between all parties to these presents,
that these articles shall be taken and construed in the
most favorable sense for the ease, comfort and advantage of the said poor Palatines intending to settle in
the country or province of North Carolina; that the
said poor Palatines doing and performing what is
intended by these presents to be done on their parts,
shall have and enjoy the benefits and advantages hereof
without any further or other demand of and from the
said Christopher de Graffenrid and Lewis Mitchell,
their heirs, executors and administrators, or any of
them; and that in case of difficulty it shall be referred to the governor of the country or province of

North Carolina, for the time being, whose order and
directions, not contrary to the intentions of these presents, shall be binding upon the said Christopher de
Graffenrid and Lewis Mitchell, his heirs, executors
and administrators, as to the said poor Palatines.

" Witness whereof the said parties to these presents
have interchangeably set their hands and seals the
day above written.

> " JOHN PHILIPS (L.S.)
> " ALEXR. CAIRNES (L.S.)
> " WHITE KENNET (L.S.)
> " JOHN CHAMBERLAIN (L.S.)
> " FREDERICK SLORE (L.S.)
> " MICAJAH PERRY (L.S.)"

" Sealed and delivered by the within named, sir
John Philips, Alexander Cairnes, White Kennet, John
Chamberlain, Frederick Slore, Micajah Perry, hav-
ing two six penny stamps.

> " In presence of us
> " WILLIAM TAYLOR,
> " JAMES DE PRATT.

" We, the within named Christopher de Graffenrid
and Lewis Mitchell, for ourselves, or heirs, executors
and administrators, do hereby covenant and agree to
and with the commissioners and trustees within written,
for and upon the like consideration mentioned, to take
and receive fifty other persons in families of the poor
Palatines, to be disposed of in like manner as the six
hundred Palatines within specified, and to have and
receive the like grants, privileges, benefits and advantages as the said six hundred Palatines have, may
or ought to have, in every article and clause within
written, and as if the said fifty Palatines had been

comprised therein, or the said articles, clauses and agreements had been here again particularly repeated and recited on to them.

"Witness our hands and seals, this 21st day of October, A.D. 1709.

"CHRISTOPHER DE GRAFFENRID,
"LEWIS MITCHELL.

"Sealed and delivered this agreement,
in the presence of
"WILLIAM TAYLOR,
"JAMES DE PRATT.

Reaching the junction of the Neuse and Trent rivers in December, 1709, the town founded was called by its founders New Berne, after the city in Switzerland whence their leaders came.

Upon this colony, there burst in September, 1711, without warning, a fearful massacre. The Tuscarora Indians, who had hitherto been friendly, were excited to war by the schemes of English adventurers plotting against the administration of Governor Hyde. John Lawson, the first historian of North Carolina, and the Surveyor General, who had boasted that the foundation of North Carolina had been laid without shedding a drop of blood, had accompanied the Baron up the Neuse river, when they were seized and condemned to death by the Indians. Lawson perished by a most cruel death, while the Baron saved his life by claiming to be the King of the Palatines, and asking his captors whether they dared to put a King to death. Before his liberation, in October, a treaty was concluded, with the stipulation that in case of war between the English and the

Indians, the Palatines would remain neutral, and that, without agreement with the Indians, no more land would be taken up.[1] Meanwhile, however, September 22d, in accordance with a plan to exterminate all settlers south of Albemarle Sound, the Indians entered the settlements simultaneously, in small parties of six or seven, and within three days slew over one hundred colonists. The provisions of the treaty preventing the Palatines from joining in the war against the Tuscaroras, that followed, alienated from them their neighbors, who were ignorant how, through their assumed neutrality, they were constantly receiving and transmitting valuable information to the English leaders. When tired of the project, with its grave responsibilities and dangers, De Graffenried sold the land of the colony which had been deeded to him, to Thomas Polloch, no attention was paid to the just claims of the Palatines. But the wrong was righted when they filed their petition stating the facts.

Before, however, such a recompense was made a portion of the colonists, in their discouragement, consisting of twelve families and fifty persons, embarked for the north, and were wrecked in April, 1714, on the Rappahanock river in Virginia. Here they were settled by Governor Spottswood on his plantation, known after them as Germanna, about twelve miles above Fredericksburg. Thither they were sent partly to work his iron furnace and partly to defend the frontier. He says that he " built a fort,

---

[1] See Graffenried's Memorandum of this Treaty, transmitted to Governor Hyde in Williamson's *North Carolina*, Appendix to Vol. I., p. 287.

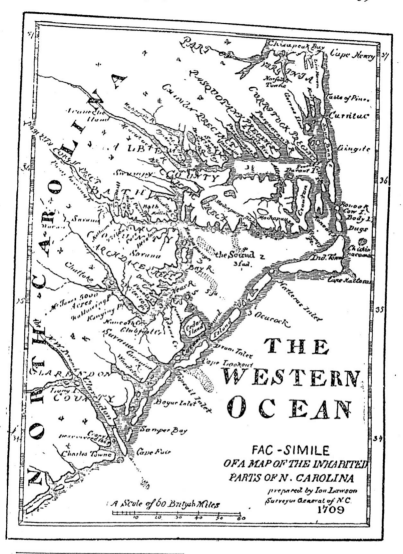

Map of North Carolina drawn by the murdered surveyor general.

and armed it with two pieces of cannon," to " awe the
struggling parties of Northern Indians, and be a *good
barrier for all that part of the country."* By successive
divisions of counties, as well as by the removal of the site
ten miles farther up the river, this colony was successively
in Spottsylvania, Orange, Culpeper and Madison counties.
Their first home was de-
scribed by Col. Byrd in
1733, as " a baker's dozen
of ruinous tenements,"
with a chapel that had
been burned by " some
pious people, with the intent to get another built
nearer their own homes."[1]
In this colony of Swiss
and Palatines was the
venerable Reformed cler-
gyman, Rev. Henry Hoe-
ger, then seventy-five
years old. An important

The Tobacco Plant.

addition was made to their number by twenty families consisting of eighty persons from the Palatinate and Alsace,
who, on their way to Pennsylvania, were detained for a
long time in England by the arrest of the captain of their
ship for debt—an incident which caused the failure of their
provisions before they reached this side of the ocean, and

[1] *Official Letters of Alex. Spottswood*, Lieutenant-Governor of Colony
of Virginia, Richmond, 1882.

Hebron Ev. Lutheran Church, Madison County, Virginia; built A.D., 1740.

the loss of many comrades from starvation. Wrecked at last in 1717 on the Virginia coast, they were sold by their captain as slaves to Governor Spottswood, who sent them to join their countrymen at Spottsylvania. This colony gave to Virginia the ancestors of the late Governor Kemper. Such was the lot of those who had been diverted, by Kocherthal's appeal, from Pennsylvania to Carolina.[1]

[1] *A Journey to the Land of Eden, by William Byrd* (1733). Reprinted, Richmond, Va , 1866, I., 59.

Arms of the Holy Roman Empire.

CHAPTER III. — THE PALATINATE EMIGRA-
TION TO NEW YORK.

Arms of the Chur-Pfaltz.

FAR more important than these southern colonies was the large emigration in 1709 to New York. Kocherthal, with his fifty-three companions, had reached New York on the last day of the year, 1708, and founded Newburg on the Hudson, called after Neuburg in the Palatinate, where more than twenty-one hundred acres were assigned them, a glebe of five hundred acres being the share of Kocherthal himself. The death of Lord Lovelace, in May, 1709, who, from his own resources, had advanced four to five hundred pounds for their support, induced Kocherthal to sail for England during that summer, in order to secure aid for his sorely pressed people. On his arrival, he was kindly heard, and his petitions granted. The ultimate decision to send a thousand of his countrymen upon the same course that he had

taken, was probably due in large measure to his presence.
As early as May 18th, Pastors Trebecco and Ruperti, in
the absence of Boehme, informed the Board of Trade,
that many of the people had expressed the desire to be
sent after their friends to New York.   But it was long

Lord Lovelace.

before their destination was fixed.   The Board inclined
towards sending them to Jamaica, to recruit the small contingent of twenty-five hundred white settlers, among the
forty thousand negroes on the island ; and many days were
spent in arranging the details for their transportation.

Bids for provisions for the use of one thousand persons on the voyage were invited, and the plan for their settlement was adopted and signed, when it was suddenly abandoned for another.

For years, the Board of Trade had been exercised with schemes for the gathering of naval supplies from the colonies. Reports in person and in writing were frequently heard from an officer especially appointed for this duty, John Bridger, who examined into the availability for this purpose, of the forests, from New England to Carolina. It was at last concluded that the pine forests of New York could be made to furnish ample tar and pitch; and that for their manufacture, the Palatines could be profitably used. With this end in view, Col. Robert Hunter was selected to succeed Lord Lovelace.

Seal and Autograph of Gen. Hunter.

Hunter wielded both pen and sword. The intimate friend of Swift and Addison and Steele, he is credited with the authorship of a classical essay on *"Enthusiasm"* once ascribed to Swift. As a Major he had been wounded at Blenheim. Appointed Lieutenant-Governor of Virginia,

he had sailed May 20, 1707, but had been captured by
privateers and carried to France, where, during the preceding winter, without suffering many serious restraints,
he had been detained as a prisoner of war. Under date
of November 30, 1709, Hunter presented an elaborate plan
for the settlement of three thousand Palatines in New York,
in reply to suggestions of the Board two months earlier,
which, after several days' discussion, was adopted. An
allowance of between three and four pounds a head was
to be made for transportation, and of forty shillings a
head for agricultural implements, while the land was to
be allotted upon the same terms as to Kocherthal and his
colonists of the preceding year. Under penalty of the
forfeiture of their patents, they were forbidden to manufacture woolen goods. Before embarking they were to be
naturalized as subjects of Great Britain. Mr. Boehme, in
a postscript to his answer to Kocherthal, has given the
regulations concerning naturalization. The person to be
naturalized must appear in England, must be furnished
with a certificate from a Protestant clergyman, endorsed
by several other witnesses, that he has received the Lord's
Supper in a Protestant church, and must take the oath of
allegiance to the Queen of England. The Board had
suggested that the Palatines would be "a good barrier
between Her Majesty's subjects and the French and their
Indians," and to this end the settlement must be either
along the Hudson or the Mohawk, where there would
also be peculiar facilities for the manufacture of turpen-
tine, tar, pitch and rosin. Forty acres, subject after seven

PRINCE GEORGE OF DENMARK, CONSORT OF QUEEN ANNE.

AFTER A PAINTING BY KNELLER.

years to a quit rent, were to be given each family " after
they shall have repaid, by the produce of their labor, the
charges the public shall be at, in settling and subsisting
them there." Because of their poverty provision is made
also for their support until they shall be able to provide
for themselves, which would not be at the soonest for less
than a year. The calculation, according to which the
Board demonstrated that the scheme would afford the Government ample remuneration for every penny expended,
read like many promising projects of more recent speculators. One man, by his own labor, they said, could
annually produce six tons of these stores. Where, however, a number were associated, the productibility of each
man was doubled. Six hundred men, therefore, might be
reasonably expected to make seven thousand tons a year.
But their eloquence with the pencil reached its climax in
the suggestion that if more would be produced by the Palatines than could be consumed in Great Britain, a profit-
able trade in these commodities with Spain and Portugal
would be assured! There was only one difficulty in the
way: The Palatines were as yet absolutely innocent of
any knowledge of this art whereby they were to enrich
the British Government! Instructors in the process were,
therefore, a necessity; and yet it was not certain that such
could be procured. Six hundred tents and the same num
ber of firearms, with bayonets, are mentioned as important
items to be included in the supplies.

By December 5th, the Board has decided that the Palatines must be settled in New York, " so as to give addi-

tional strength and security to that Province, not only with regard to the French of Canada, but against any insurrection of the scattered nations of Indians in these parts, and, in process of time, by intermarrying with the neighboring Indians (as the French do), they may be capable of rendering very great service to Her Majesty's subjects there; and not only very much promote the Fur Trade, but, likewise, the increase of Naval Stores." From Hunter's report it appears that not only the settlements on the Piscataqua River, or New Hampshire, but that even those on the Kennebec in Maine, were under discussion as suitable homes.

Meanwhile an instrument revised by Attorney-General Montague, entitled "*Covenant for the Palatines' Residence and Employment in New York,*" was subscribed by each of the responsible emigrants after it had first been translated and read to them in German. To this document, and to the fact that it had been understood when signed, Governor Hunter appealed when, in 1720, he appeared in the presence of the elder Weiser before the Board of Trade, to answer the charge of having wronged the Palatines, and to meet their claim for possessions in the Schoharie district. It certainly binds the Palatines very tightly, and, although they heard it in their own language, their anticipations of the ease with which its conditions could be fulfilled when they would reach America, were such that they probably did not consider all that was involved.

COVENANT FOR THE PALATINES' RESIDENCE AND
EMPLOYMENT IN NEW YORK.[1]

" Whereas, we the underwritten persons, natives of
the Lower Palatinate of the Rhine, have been subsisted, maintained and supported ever since our arrival
in this kingdom by the great and Christian charity of
Her Majesty, the Queen, and of many of her good
subjects; and, whereas Her Majesty has been graciously pleased to order and advance a loan for us, and
on our behalf of several very considerable sums towards the transporting, maintaining and settling of us
and our respective families in Her Majesty's Province
of New York in America, and towards the employing of us upon lands, for that intent and purpose to be
allotted to us, in the production and manufacture of all
manner of naval stores, to the evident benefit and advantage of us, and our respective families, and whereas
Her Majesty has been likewise graciously pleased
to give Her royal orders to the Hon. Col. Robert
Hunter, who has now Her Majesty's commission to be
Captain General and Governor in Chief of the said
Province, and to all Governors of the said Province
for the time being, that as soon as we shall have made
good and repaid to Her Majesty, Her heirs or successors, out of the produce of our labors in the manufactures we are to be employed in, the full sum or
sums of money in which we already are or shall become, indebted to Her Majesty, by the produce of our
labor in all manner of naval stores on the lands to that
end to be allotted to us, that then he, the said Col. Robert Hunter, or the Governor or Governors of the said

---

[1] *Documents pertaining to Colonial History of New York*, V., 121 sqq.

Province for the time being shall give and grant to us and our heirs forever, to our own use and benefit, the said lands so allotted as aforesaid, to the proportion or amount of forty acres to each person, free from all taxes, quit rents or other manner of services for seven years, from the date of such grant, and afterwards subjected only to such reservations as are accustomed and in use in that Her Majesty's said Province.

" Now KNOW ALL MEN by these Presents, that we, the said underwritten persons, in a grateful sense, just regard and due consideration of the premises, do hereby severally for ourselves, our heirs, executors and administrators, covenant, promise and grant to and with the Queen's most excellent Majesty, Her heirs and successors, that we with our respective families will settle ourselves in such place or places as shall be allotted to us in the Province of New York on the Continent of America, and abide and continue resident upon the lands so to be allotted to us as aforesaid, in such bodies or societies as shall be thought useful or necessary either for carrying on the manufacture of things proper for naval stores or for the defence of us and the rest of Her Majesty's subjects against the French or any other of Her Majesty's enemies, and that we will not, upon any account, or any manner of pretext, quit or desert the said Province, without leave from the Governor of the said Province first had and obtained for so doing, but that we will, to our utmost power, employ and occupy ourselves and our respective families in the producing and manufacturing of all manner of naval stores upon the lands so to be allotted us, or on such other lands as shall be thought more proper for that purpose, and not concern ourselves in working up or making things belonging to the woolen manufacture, but behave ourselves in all things as becomes dutiful and loyal subjects, and grateful and faithful servants to Her Majesty, her heirs and successors, paying all due obedience to the said Hon. Col. Robert Hunter or to the Governor or Governors of the said Province for the time being, and to all magistrates and other officers who shall from time to time be legally appointed and set over us; and towards repayment of Her Majesty, her heirs and successors, all such sums of money, as she or they shall at any time disburse for our support and maintenance, till we can reap the benefit of the produce of our labors, we shall permit all naval stores by us manufactured to be put into Her Majesty's storehouses which shall be for this purpose provided, under the care of a commissary, who is to keep a faithful account of the goods which shall be so delivered, and we shall allow out of the neat produce thereof so much to be paid Her Majesty, her heirs and successors, as upon a fair account shall appear to have been disbursed for subsistence of us, or providing necessaries for our families. In witness, etc."

The precise date of the sailing from England of the colonists is in doubt. Conrad Weiser says: "About Christmas Day, we embarked." A contemporary German account says that they were on the sea from Christmas to Easter. Henry Bendysh, who had the contract to transport them, agreed that January 2d should be the date for their sailing. But the Queen had not actually signed the instructions to Hunter, until January 26th. Pastor Trebecco's sermon before the embarkation was preached on

January 20th. As was frequently the case, there may
have been considerable delay at Portsmouth after the embarkation, and the vessels may have gradually received
their passengers, so that the discrepancy of a month may
be readily explained.

A like diversity occurs with respect to the number of the
emigrants. Conrad Weiser's figure is four thousand,

Savoy Palace and Chapel.

which harmonizes with the statement of his father and
Scheff to the Board of Trade in 1720. Bendysh con-
tracted to carry in ten ships about three thousand three
hundred. General Nicholson testified in 1720 that the
number was about three thousand two hundred. A con-

temporary German account fixes it as three thousand and eighty-six; and all other statements we have noted give the estimate of three thousand.

With the emigrants, Pastor Kocherthal sailed on his return. A Reformed student of theology, John Frederick Hager, whose name is almost that of the Virginia Reformed pastor, received Episcopal ordination in England, and sailed in this expedition, as a missionary of the Society for the Propagation of the Gospel in Foreign Parts. A very important member of the party was John Conrad Weiser, Sr., a widower accompanied by eight of his children, one of whom, a boy then twelve years old, was to become one of the most prominent factors in the history of colonial Pennsylvania, and the ancestor of Governor J. A. Schultz and of the first Speaker of the House of Representatives of the United States, and his brother, Major General Peter Muhlenberg. With them also were the great grandfather of William C. Bouck, Governor of the State of New York, from 1843 to 1845, and the ancestor of the Revolutionary hero, General Herkheimer.

No artist has painted the embarkation of the Palatines on those ten vessels; and, yet, would not the theme be just as fruitful, and the subject as worthy, as that of the Pilgrims from Rotterdam? Many go forth to meet the trials of the new world, as veterans, who, by the desolations of war that had raged around them, from their earliest years, in their fatherland, have been well prepared for the post they are to fill, as a wall of protection to the English settlers against the Indians. In his hand, each of them

carries a small prayer-book, provided, at the expense of
Queen Anne, by the London German pastors. Opening the
volume with much veneration, we find there the "Sermon
on the Mount," and five prayers. One of these prayers
that served to guide the devotion of many a distressed
heart, amidst the terrors of the storm, the horrors of dis-
ease, the loss of loved ones, and the struggle with death,
during the passage that followed, may be appropriately
introduced:

"ETERNAL AND MERCIFUL GOD, Whose goodness
is every morning new, and Whose faithfulness is great
towards us, poor men, we praise, we worship, we
adore Thee, and from our hearts thank Thee, this
morning, that Thou hast so graciously protected us
during the past night, not dealing with us after our
sins, but showing towards us great patience and calling us to repentance, faith and eternal life. Of all
such blessings for body and for soul, we are unworthy,
O Lord. We confess before Thee our sins, that have
been committed against Thee often and in many ways.
Lord, be merciful unto us, and forgive our guilt according to Thy great mercy, for Christ's sake. Grant
us also an earnest hatred of all sins, and renew us, by
Thy Holy Spirit, that henceforth we may not be the
servants of sin, but may walk in righteousness and
holiness all the days of our lives, since Thou hast
redeemed us through Christ, and bought us to be Thine
own. Into thy faithful hands, then, O God, we commend our bodies and souls, and all that we have and
are. Bless us especially with spiritual blessings, that
acknowledging Thee more and more, we may love

and hold fast to Thy Word. Bless us also with
temporal blessings, granting us health and peace and
provision for our bodily needs, and caring for us and
ours in all things. Unto Thee we commit all our
ways. Rule and direct us all, as in Thy good counsel,
Thou knowest it will be best for us."

The sermon preached by Mr. Trebecco in St. Cathe-
rine's church, London, January 20th, to many of the
emigrants, vividly recalls the entire situation. No more

Trebecco Preaching to the Palatines in Savoy Chapel.

appropriate text could have been chosen. It was Deut. 8 :
1–3 : " All the commandments which I command you this
day, shall ye observe and do, that ye may live and multiply
and go in and possess the land which the Lord sware unto
your fathers. And thou shalt remember all the way
which the Lord thy God led thee these forty years in the
wilderness, to humble thee, and to prove thee, to know
what was in thy heart, whether thou wouldst keep his commandments or no. And he humbled thee and suffered
thee to hunger, and fed thee with manna, which thou

knewest not, neither did thy fathers know; that he might make thee know that man doth not live by bread only, but by every word that proceedeth out of the mouth of God doth man live." After explaining the passage, he continued:

"My beloved Palatines, you can easily see that I have selected this text carefully that you may remember it on your voyage, and learn to make a proper use of your condition as pilgrims. While in many particulars your pilgrimage is very unlike that of the children of Israel, there are still many others in which there is a great resemblance. The dissimilarity consists in the fact that the departure of the children of Israel was a work of God, in obedience to his express command, while yours from your Fatherland, was in many respects, I fear, a work of man, who deceived you with vain hopes of obtaining great things, extensive lands, rich property, etc. Some were indeed forced to emigrate, from their extreme necessities; but others, from needless, aye, I may say, sinful curiosity. As therefore, the beginning was mostly human, and in many instances sinful, so also the progress of events have shown that, for the most part, you have not reached the end you were seeking. Many are now contemplating a return to Germany, while to those who intend to go to the West Indies we wish only God's blessing.

"But there are more circumstances that enable me to speak of *The Similarity between your Journey and that of the Children of Israel in the Wilderness.* First, it was not without God's will, which often brings punishment and just judgment upon the world, that

this has happened. Farther, beneath these chastise-
ments, the goodness of God may be remarkably traced.
You Palatines have many reasons for acknowledgment
that God has wonderfully helped you thus far, and in
a strange land has fed you with bread from Heaven,
and refreshed you with water out of the rock, by
opening the heart of our Most Gracious Queen, to
bestow upon you such remarkable generosity, and
awakening the sympathy and liberality of many of
Her esteemed subjects. Nor should you forget that
God did not leave you without pastors to care for your
souls. A special Divine Providence has sustained you,
like the children of Israel, so that in these extremely
hard times, for many long months you have had all
your wants supplied. Then, too, you are alike in the
difficulty of the way, which you have experienced,
and (God help you!) you must yet experience.
Those who, like me, have looked after your interests,
as both superintendents and servants, have had our
sympathies and anxieties greatly exercised at the
thought of the large number of people, for whom we
had to care, with their many sicknesses and necessities, and miseries, from which many deaths, and other
calamities have followed. Many alas! merited these
punishments by their sins and vices. For your humili-
ation, I must say, that in nothing are you more like
the children of Israel, than in your sins, your unbelief,
your disobedience, your surroundings, your impa-
tience, your discontent, your fleshy lusts, etc. No injustice would be done, if, like Moses, I were to call
you an obstinate, and stiff-necked people, who walk
after the thoughts of your hearts, and will not learn
the ways of God, even when He has chastened you

sore. For as you are like the children of Israel in
your sins, so also are you in your punishments. This
explains why it is that there are among you so many
widows and widowers and orphans; although God has
taken from you tender children, and provided for them
far better than you ever attended.

" Now, why has God let all this come upon you?
For this reason, says the text, ' to humble. thee, and
to prove thee, and to know what was in thy heart.'
Many a one has thought that these intentions and purposes were the very best, who now sees, after God has
thus proved him, that there was much that he lacked,
that his former life was a failure, that he was seeking
only earthly things, and was sinning grievously against
God and his neighbor, and that he has been untrue
even to himself. O that God would humble you, that
you would fall at His feet, and heartily pray for for-
giveness, and that He turn away the punishments
you have heretofore experienced ! * * * * *

" There is an anxiety that disturbs many with respect to their religion. They imagine that they cannot live in a land where they cannot attend public
worship in their mother tongue. We would not de-
preciate the peculiar favor of God that preserves to
one such a privilege. But where this is impossible,
and one is well-grounded in his Christian faith, and
in regard to all matters of faith there is freedom of
conscience, no Christian should have any scruples of
conscience about attending service in another language which he has learned, particularly if such service be held in Protestant and Evangelical churches.
Such is the case with your friends in Ireland and elsewhere. A Christian proves all things, and holds fast

to that which is good. We do not deny that in the so-called Christendom, the light of God's Word shines more brightly in one communion than another, and that we must not yield the least that concerns the pure and saving truth. But we oppose the fearful prejudices and false ideas of religion, that prevail to-day, and divide Christendom, and should not be judged otherwise than according to the meaning of Christ, 2 Cor. 4 : 20.

"Pray God, therefore, for grace and a true change of mind! Then will He regard your misery, and remove your want, and care for you both in body and in soul, and redeem you from all evil, and, after your pilgrimage has been finished in this sorrowful world He will at last grant to us all, who have placed our hopes upon Him, and have followed Him here, eternal peace, joy and salvation, through Jesus Christ, to Whom, with the Father and the Holy Ghost, be glory forever. *Amen.*"

CHAPTER IV.—ON THE OCEAN.

A " Compass rose," from an old chart.

HERE we may properly interrupt the narrative to consider some of the perils and hardships that were to be apprehended in the voyage. Many of them this company of emigrants were to suffer ; but while they were spared from others, their countrymen who followed, the fathers of many of us, were not equally fortunate. Always uncertain was the length of the voyage. Pastor Kocherthal in his plea for Carolina, says that, when everything is favorable, the voyage from England thither could be made in six or five, and even, in exceptional cases, in four weeks ; but that, under other circumstances, it might consume half a year. Before steam was used in navigation, the course might be interrupted by an indefinite calm. The imperfect knowledge of hydrography prevented them from taking advantage of well-defined ocean currents, and the lack of sufficient charts and light-houses rendered approach to the coast exceedingly difficult. The determination of the place of the ship, when compared with the results of the more exact methods of to-day, was scarcely more than guess-work. Men raised in our busy age would be worn out with the protracted delays of weeks and sometimes months, before the vessel in which they embarked, started, and would live over again the pains of Tantalus, while provoking calms kept the vessels from shore already seen, or contrary winds drove it far out to sea, after the goal of their long wandering had been almost attained.

The voyages of William Penn were made under the most favorable circumstances, and yet his first to America in 1682 consumed two months; his return in 1684, seven weeks; and his second trip to America in 1699, more than three months. Readers of Mr. Sachse's "History of the German Pietists," will recall the fact that the emigrants on the *Sarah Maria* were on board from February 13th to June 19th. More than a generation later, we find the Salzburgers making their way to the coast of Georgia, one transport leaving England at the very beginning of January, 1734, and reaching Charleston, March 18th (two months and a-half) ; and another leaving the coast of England, October 28, 1735, and reaching Charleston, February 15th, 1736 (three months and eighteen days). Henry Melchior Muhlenberg in 1742, left the coast of England, June 13th, and did not set foot upon

solid land until September 23d, a voyage of three months
and ten days. Pastor Handschuh, who arrived in 1748,
went on board September 25, 1747, but because of an
accident to the vessel, the final start was not taken until
January 14th, and Philadelphia was not reached until
April 5th, six months and ten days from the time of embarkation.

With half the shipping engaged in illegitimate business,
as smuggling, privateering and piracy, the risk of sailing
without a convoy of men-of-war was great, while the difficulty of securing them was another source of vexatious delays. Cases of piracy and mutiny are frequent subjects of
consideration in the Minutes of the Provincial Council of
Pennsylvania. The coasts of the Carolinas and Georgia
were favorite lurking places for pirates.

Their exploits have been recounted in a monograph published a few years ago under the authority of Johns Hop-
kins University : " *The Carolina Pirates* and *Colonial
Commerce*, 1670–1740," 1894. Beginning as privateers
against the Spanish dominions in America, not only with
the authority, but the very decided encouragement of King
Charles II., the trade was so well learned by a host of adventurers, that when peace between the two countries came,
their efforts were directed towards an illegitimate continu-
ance of the same work. The doubtful compliment of
Scaliger shows the extent of this crime in the English
colonies : "*Nulli melius piraticam exercent quam Angli.*"
It is alleged that for years their chief victims were still
Spanish, and that, in this course, they were not without

Blackbeard the Pirate.

(From a contemporary print.)

much sympathy from the inhabitants of the Southern colonies, as they looked upon them as some protection against the dread of a violation of treaty rights by the Spanish. However this may be, the pirates did not scruple long about preying upon whatever commerce was within reach, without regard to the flag under which it floated. During the administration of Governor Craven, 1711–13, it was estimated that no less than 1,500 men engaged in this business, infested the coast. Of these 800 had their headquarters on the island of Providence, while the mouth of the Cape Fear River was the next chief place of resort. "They swept the coast from Newfoundland to South America, plundering their prizes at sea, or carrying them into Cape Fear or Providence as best suited their convenience."[1] In June, 1718, Edward Thatch (Teach) known as "Blackbeard," appeared off Charleston, with four vessels, the largest of forty guns, and with four hundred men in his fleet, and remaining there for days, captured all the vessels entering or going from the harbor. Sending a boat to Charleston, he forced the Governor of South Carolina, to furnish him with necessary medical supplies, under the menace of the execution of certain prominent citizens whom he had captured. Thatch, whose depredations extended to the approaches to Philadelphia, was captured shortly after this bold move by an expedition sent against him by Governor Spottswood, of Virginia.

---

[1] Interesting details in "*The History of South Carolina under the Proprietory Government*," by Edward MacCrady, New York, 1897, especially Chapters XXVI. and XXVII.

" Hardly a ship goes to sea," writes the Governor of South Carolina, " but falls into the hands of pirates."

Major Stede Bonnet, a man of liberal education, good family and wealth with a creditable military record, was led, by some strange infatuation, after he had passed the prime of life, to embark in this same career of crime, and to rival Thatch in the terror he struck along the entire Atlantic coast. In the summer of 1718, he took thirty-eight vessels, among them several in the Delaware Bay. On September 27, 1718, a desperate naval battle was fought at Cape Fear by two vessels despatched thither, under Col. William Rhett, by the Governor of South Carolina, and the ship of Bonnet. He and his men were captured, but not until after five hours hard fighting, and the loss by the Carolinians of twelve killed and twenty-eight wounded. Their trial had scarcely begun before the alarm was sounded that another body of pirates was at the entrance of Charleston Harbor. Hastily fitting up another expedition, in which the vessel captured from Bonnet was utilized, the Governor undertook the command in person, and went forth with four vessels and twenty-eight guns. The pirates were surprised, and captured, but only after a battle almost equally severe to that at Cape Fear. In one of their two ships, were found 106 convicts and " covenant servants," en route to Maryland and Virginia, whom the pirates were holding as prisoners. Worley the piratical chief killed in this engagement, is said to have terrorized the coasts in the vicinity of New York and Philadelphia. In November,

1718, there were in Charleston no less than forty-five
pirates executed.

In the first volume of " *The American Weekly Mer-
cury*," the first paper published in the City of Philadelphia,
and which is being rendered accessible by the photographic
reproduction of our skillful fellow-member, Julius F.

A Battle with Pirates.

Sachse, the accounts of the depredations of pirates, from
Newfoundland to Brazil, are prominent items of news.
May 17, 1720, tells of the capture of a certain Capt. Knot,
with his vessel by 148 pirates, who was released, but compelled to take on board as passengers eight men, who

conveyed in this way their treasure of 1,500 pounds sterling to Virginia, but were there arrested and hung. April 7th, a ship has just arrived in New York, that had been robbed by pirates in the Barbadoes. April 14th, a Philadelphia vessel has been robbed on her way to the Barbadoes. May 5th, an engagement with pirates off the Barbadoes, in which they escape. Rescue of a vessel from pirates, near Boston. May 19th, Capt. Thorpe of Philadelphia, captured by Spanish privateers, off the capes of Virginia. June 30th, account of depredations on the coasts of Guinea. July 14th, Spanish privateers and pirates on the Virginia capes. Release of 70 prisoners taken by them. Corpses of those they had killed discovered. September 1st, capture of a ship by a pirate off the banks of Newfoundland. Ten thousand pounds sterling thrown overboard. Rumor that the Fort of St. John has been taken by pirates, and all the fishing vessels there destroyed. September 8th, the brigantine " Essex" reaches Salem, after being captured by pirates, sixty leagues east of the banks of Newfoundland by two vessels, one of 25 guns and 100 men, and the other of 10 guns. Just before this capture another vessel had fallen into their hands. September 22d relates a feat of remarkable audacity. Pirates in a small sloop of 12 guns, and with 160 men had entered Trespassy, and taken possession of the harbor with all the vessels there, including 22 sail. The ship carpenters were pressed into the work of making such repairs as the pirates desired. Thirty French and English ships had been destroyed on the banks. The week before, they had been at Ferryland, where two

A R T I C L E S of Agreement, *made* this 10th day of October *in the Year of our Lord* 1695. *between the Right Honourable* Richard *Earl of* Bellomont *of the one part, and* Robert Levingston *Efq; and Capt.* William Kid *of the other part.*

WHEREAS the faid Capt. *William Kid* is defirous of obtaining a Commiffion as Captain of a Private Man of War in order to take Prizes from the King's Enemies, and otherways to annoy them ; and whereas certain Perfons did fome time fince depart from *New-England, Rode-Ifland, New-York*, and other parts in *America* and elfewhere, with an intention to become Pirates, and to commit Spoils and Depredations, againft the Laws of Nations, in the *Red-Sea* or elfewhere, and to return with fuch Goods and Riches as they fhould get, to certain places by them agreed upon ; of which faid Perfons and Places the faid Capt. *Kid* hath notice, and is defirous to fight with and fubdue the faid Pirates, as alfo all other Pirates with whom

---

Facsimile of heading of the original Broadside, now in collection of the Historical Society of Pennsylvania

vessels were burnt. Although they had had two days' notice of their approach, and there were in the harbor 1,200 men, with 40 guns, all were paralyzed with fear, and unable to make a resistance. Other notices of depredations are recorded on October 27th, November 10th, November 24th, and December 8th.

The evil must have been indeed extreme, when in 1697, Penn wrote to Deputy Governor Markham of Pennsylvania charging the Provincial Council with having "not only countenanced, but actually encouraged piracy." The Council indignantly protested that no piratical vessels had ever been harbored, much less encouraged in Pennsylvania, and make a public proclamation announcing the charge, and urging all magistrates to prove its incorrectness by a rigid enforcement of the laws guarding against such offence. On Penn's return, we are told that his first act on reassuming control of the government, was to reconvene the Assembly "for the express and only purpose of reënacting two measures, which in his opinion, the existing state of affairs rendered imperative." The first of these was "An Act against Pirates and Privateers."[1]

The notorious depredations of Capt. Kidd extended into the Delaware Bay. Penn's charge against the Provincial Council must be read in the light of the fact that Kidd had embarked upon his career as a privateersman with a commission from the Governor of New York, the Earl of Bella-

---

[1] *Duke of York's Laws*, etc. Harrisburg, 1879. Historical Notes on Early Government and Legislative Councils by Benjamin W. Nead, pp. 573 sqq.

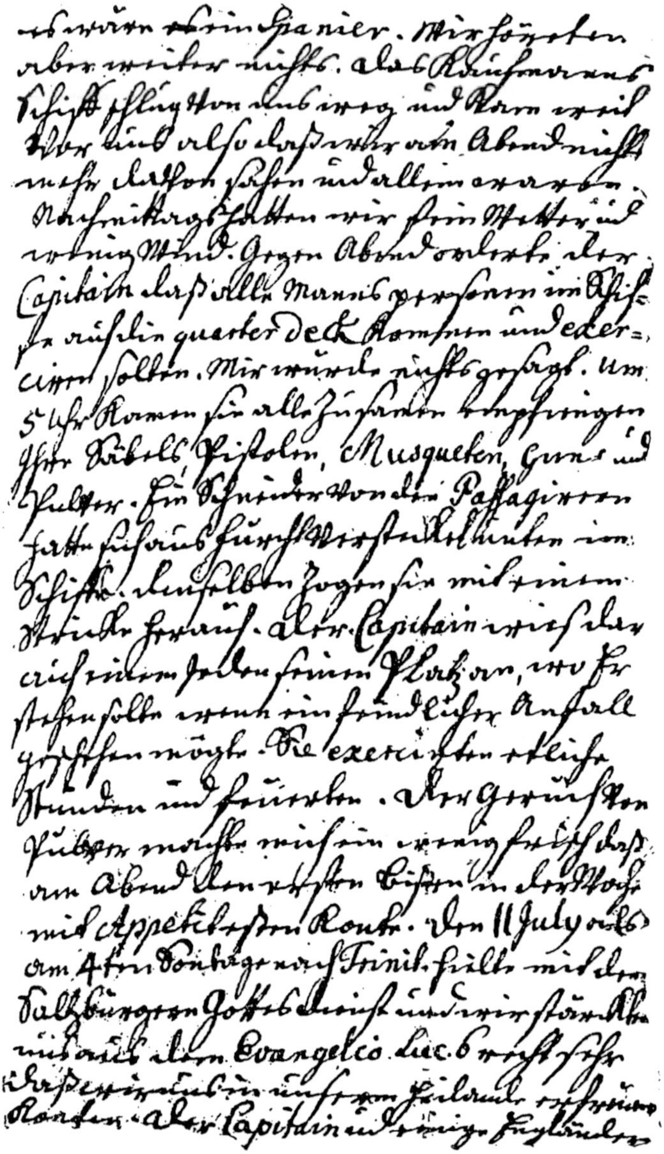

Page from Muhlenberg's Diary of Voyage in 1742. (In Archives of Theological Seminary, Mt. Airy, Philadelphia.)

Henry Melchior Muhlenberg

mont, who had to meet the charge that his appointment as Governor was determined by his purpose to encourage piracy. It was the irony of fate that Kidd was to be condemned and executed in 1700[1] under Bellamy himself. Indignant as were his protests that he was guiltless of encouraging piracy, the commission of 1697 tells its own tale.

While on his way to England in 1718, to present the grievances of the Palatines, John Conrad Weiser, Sr., was captured shortly after leaving Philadelphia, and most cruelly handled. The same year King George I. made a proclamation, offering an amnesty to all pirates abandoning their trade. One of the most interesting incidents in Mr. Sachse's book is the description by Daniel Falkner[2] of the sea fight with the three French vessels during the voyage hither of German pietists in 1694. Mr. Brickenstein, in his account of the First Sea Congregation of the Moravians, has given a graphic description of the manner in which an attack of a privateer was repulsed by the forty-nine hats of peaceful and unarmed brethren seen upon the deck. A similar ruse was attempted by the vessel that brought Muhlenberg to this country in 1742, when cannon were loaded and the drummers beat their drums. We present a facsimile of a page of his diary where he refers to this incident:

---

[1] See *Commission*; also *Full Account of Proceedings against Capt. Cook*, London, 170.

[2] The finding of the original manuscript in the archives at Halle, shows that this report was written by Johann Gottfried Seelig, a former Secretary to Rev. Philip Jacob Spener, who came over with the Kelpins community, and not by Falkner, as has been heretofore assumed.—J. F SACHSE.

" It was a Spaniard. But we heard nothing more. The merchant's vessel beat off from us, and so far outran us, that by evening we no longer saw anything of it, and were alone. In the afternoon we had fine weather and little wind. Towards evening, the captain ordered that every male person in the vessel should come on the quarter deck and drill. Nothing was said to me. About five o'clock they all came together, received their sabres, pistols, muskets, guns and powder. A tailor, one of the passengers, had, out of fear, concealed himself in the hold. Him they drew out with a rope. Thereupon the captain showed each one the place where he should stand, in case a hostile attack should be made. They drilled for several hours and fired. The smell of powder freshened me up a little, so that in the evening I could, for the first time in the week, eat a bit with an appetite. On July 11th, it being the fourth Sunday after Trinity, I held divine service with the Salzburgers, and we greatly refreshed ourselves from the Gospel of Luke 6, so that we were able to rejoice in our Saviour. The captain and several Englishmen. [1]

The imminence of this danger to the Palatines, in this and subsequent voyages, may be inferred from the scheme that may still be read, prepared in 1711 for Gov. Hunter for guarding the coasts " against the insults of French privateers," in which they are designated as " swarms which every summer infest our coasts, where they not only take vast numbers of our vessels, but have plundered several small towns and villages."

---

[1] From the diary of Muhlenberg, while on his voyage to America, 1742.

The long voyages rendered it difficult to carry sufficient provisions and to keep them in good condition. Contractors were no less dishonest in those days than in our own, and where the emigrants were carried at the lowest figures every effort was made to economize in the quality and quantity of the food. Extraordinary delays meant hunger, if not starvation. The bill of fare, with meat four times, and fish three times a week, recorded by Pastorius, as that of the vessel in which he sailed, bears a wonderful contrast with that of a Cunarder or North German Lloyd of to-day; but when his passage was only six pounds sterling for himself, and twenty-two rix-dollars for each domestic, he received an equivalent for what he paid.[1] Often the drinking water failed. Muhlenberg's description of the eagerness of the passengers on his vessel to catch a few drops of rain from passing showers; of the rush of the children to collect the water escaping from the joints of the casks just received from a passing ship, and the desperate ingenuity of the rats when they emptied the vinegar bottles by drawing the corks and using their tails as absorbents of the precious fluid, give some impression of the extremity to which emigrants were sometimes put.[2]

Often the captains and sailors were rough, domineering, cruel, and emigrants were crowded in with vermin-covered and profane fellow-passengers. Pastor Handschuh speaks of those with whom he sailed being packed together like herring. "Like herring," also Muhlenberg says, the

---

[1] Pastorius, *Beschreibung von Pennsyl.*, Crefeld, 1884. (Reprint.)
[2] Mann's *Life of H. M. Mühlenberg*, Philadelphia, 1887, pp. 48 sqq.

people slept in the cabin of the packet that carried him from Savannah to Philadelphia. Casper Wistar writes in 1732 of a ship that had been twenty-four weeks at sea, that had lost one hundred of its one hundred and fifty passengers by starvation, the rats and mice having been caught to satisfy the hunger, and the price of a mouse fixed at half a gulden, and whose survivors were all thrown into prison for the debts of the living and the dead.[1] Another vessel, seventeen weeks on the way, lost sixty of its passengers, and brought the rest to land in a condition of extreme enfeeblement. The experience of the Palatines, wrecked on the coast of Virginia in 1717, has been already related. In December, 1738, a ship was wrecked at Block Island, that had sailed with four hundred Palatines, all of whom save one hundred and five had died of fever, while fifteen more died shortly after landing, the entire loss being over seventy-seven per cent., and the bad condition of the water taken in at Rotterdam being assigned as the cause of the mortality. Fifty survivors out of four hundred, the most of the deaths having been from starvation, was the record of a vessel that arrived at Philadelphia in 1745. Bread had been distributed every two weeks in such scant amounts that many consumed it in less than half the time it was intended to last, when, if they had money, they bought meal and wine at exorbitant rates, but, otherwise, were left to their fate. The deaths in fifteen vessels in 1738, are estimated by one writer as sixteen hundred, while

---

[1] Letter in *Sammlung Ausserlessener Materiel zum Bau des Reichs Gottes*, Leipzig, 1733, Vol. IX. p. 512.

Christopher Saur regards two thousand no exaggeration. On the ship that carried Henry Keppele that year two hundred and fifty died, exclusive of the victims of the voyage after landing.

With no attention paid to the sanitation of ships, ship fever was no unusual scourge. A medical commission appointed by the Provincial Council of Pennsylvania in 1754, made a full report concerning the diseases produced and propagated from the overcrowded vessels of Palatines, as follows:

"The diseases to which all places are liable from foreigners brought among them in crowded vessels are: first, fevers from a foul air, which is common to these ships; secondly, these fevers aggravated by other causes on board the ships or in houses where too many of the sick have been kept together in small and close rooms; thirdly, fevers from infectious matter brought on board the ships from other places. That you may be the better able to judge of the means necessary for preventing these diseases, we think it will not be improper first to say something of their causes, and then to show by facts where the danger of infection from them lies.

"The steam of bilge water and the breath of great numbers of people betwixt the decks of a ship make the air moist and in some degree putrid, and, like that of moist and boggy places, will produce fevers on persons that are a long time in them, but these fevers are not contagious and require no other precaution, but separating the sick and keeping them in places well aired and cleaned.

" But when to this state of the air, any considerable degree of animal putrefaction is added, either from uncleanness, flukes, etc., or too great a confinement of the air itself, it then produces a fever different in its symptoms from the former, malignant in its nature and contagious. Military hospitals afford us daily instances of the mildest fevers being by these causes changed into malignant and contagious ones, and prove how dangerous it is for many sick persons to be kept together in the manner we found the Palatines in the two houses mentioned to you in our last report. But the most fatal circumstances attending contagious fevers are when persons infected by them in jails and other places (where the cause has been long gaining force) communicate them to the passengers of a crowded ship in the beginning of a summer voyage, where, from the number of the sick, heat of the weather and frequent calms, they rage with such violence and continue so long that every part of the ship imbibes the poison, and will retain it for a considerable time, after both goods and people have been taken out of her. The vessels of this port that bring people from these places usually land them in a neighboring government and have not been sufficiently suspected of danger as we are persuaded the following facts will convince you:

" Captain Arthur, who was then a mate of Captain Davis, told us that in the year 1741 they took in a parcel of convicts from the Dublin Gaol and other servants from the city. Soon after the people on board were seized with fevers, which few escaped, so that they were in great distress from the number of the sick during the whole voyage. Where the people were landed we did not inquire; but this ship, after they were out, was brought to Hamilton's wharf, and from thence carried to Thomas Penrose's to be repaired. Soon after her coming to the wharf seven persons in the family of Anthony Morris, the elder, and several in the house of Anthony Morris, the younger, were seized with putrid bilious fever, and seventeen of Mr. Penrose's family who had been on board the ship, were likewise affected with the same fever, and also sundry persons in every part of that neighborhood where the ballast of the ship was thrown. This fever afterwards raged through the city to the loss of many of its valuable inhabitants.

* * * * * * * * *

"Ever since the middle of September there have been a few putrid fevers in this city, which we believe were not owing to the climate but to an infection either brought or generated among us by foreigners. The first of these certainly did not come from the Palatines, but whether they have added fresh fuel and continued them, we cannot determine: however this, we are convinced of (and which we have never till lately suspected) that the true state of the Palatine ships is too often concealed from the physicians who visit them, in such a manner that it is impossible to discover it from anything they can see on board.

"There have been diseases of the same nature with these mentioned at other times in the city, but we did not know anything relating to them that would make their enumeration necessary; therefore, shall conclude with only taking the liberty to assure you we are,

"Sir, Your most obedient humble servants,

"THOMAS GREEME,
"THOMAS BOND.

"December 2, 1754."

To this is added the melancholy postscript:

"The Council, for their further information, sent for Jacob Shoemaker, the man who has the care of the Strangers' Burying Ground, and ordered him to deliver in upon oath the number of Palatines buried there, which he did as follows:

"An account of the Palatines buried this year:

"For Alexander Stedman........ 62
"For Henry Keppelly........... 39
"For Benjamin Shoemaker...... 57
"For Daniel Benezet........... 87
"For Michael Hillegass.........   8
                              ____
"Total.................. ...253

"Jacob Shoemaker upon his affirmation saith the above account of burials since the 14th of September last is exact and true from his book and the account of coffins, except those from Michael Hillegass, which he thinks may be six or eight more, and some to be buried this day, November 14, 1754."[1]

This indicates that the average mortality of Palatines just arrived, at the port of Philadelphia, continued throughout an entire summer to be from eight to nine per day.

Nevertheless, it must not be inferred that such was the universal experience of the emigrant vessels. Instances are on record where vessels filled with German emigrants brought every passenger to land; but the mortality from small-pox on the ship in which William Penn came hither in 1682, shows that the utmost precautions could not entirely exclude such perils. Well has the late Dr. Mann,

---

[1] *Pennsylvania Colonial Records*, VI., 173 sqq.

Henry Keppele

in his "Life of Muhlenberg," designated the vessels of those days, as instead of the floating palaces of to-day, being "combinations of floating fortresses, floating prisons and floating hospitals."

Such trustworthy witnesses as John Wesley, Baron von Reck, Pastor Boltzius of the Salzburgers and Henry Melchior Muhlenburg have given graphic descriptions of the numerous, fierce and protracted storms they encountered, and the varied conduct of the passengers in the presence of danger, as the prospect of immediate death, while sails were tearing and masts breaking and the vessel giving every indication that all was lost, unmanned the bravest and called forth shrieks of horror from some, but still others, elsewhere most timid, met the crisis with an indescribable composure, arising from their conviction that their Father in Heaven held the waves of the sea in the hollow of His hands. It was such heaven-born peace, displayed by his German fellow-passengers, that astonished Wesley, and, according to his own confession, led him to an entirely new conception of the Christian life.

REV. JOHN WESLEY'S JOURNAL. [1]

"*Saturday, January 17, 1736.*—Many people were very impatient at the contrary wind. At seven in the evening they were quieted by a storm. It rose higher and higher till nine. About nine the sea broke over us from stem to stern; burst through the windows of the state cabin, where three or four of us

---

[1] The works of Rev. John Wesley, M.A., London, 1829, I., 20–23.

were, and covered us all over, though a bureau sheltered me from the main shock. About eleven I lay
down in the great cabin, and in a short time fell
asleep, though very uncertain whether I should wake
alive, and much ashamed of my unwillingness to
die. O how pure in heart must he be, who would
rejoice to appear before God at a moment's warning!
Toward morning, ' He rebuked the winds and the
sea, and there was a great calm.'

" *Sunday 18.*—We returned God thanks for our de-
liverance, of which a few seemed duly sensible. But
the rest (among whom were most of the sailors) denied we had been in any danger. I could not have
believed that so little good would have been done by
the terror they were in before. But it cannot be that
they should long obey God from fear, who are deaf to
the motives of love.

" *Friday 23.*—In the evening another storm began, in the morning it increased, so that they were
forced to let the ship drive. I could not but say to
myself, ' How is it that thou hast no faith?' being still
unwilling to die. About one in the afternoon, almost
as soon as I had stepped out of the great cabin door,
the sea did not break as usual, but came with a full,
smooth tide over the side of the ship. I was vaulted
over with water in a moment, and so stunned, that I
scarce expected to lift up my head again, till the sea
should give up her dead. But thanks be to God, I received no hurt at all. About midnight the storm
ceased.

" *Sunday 25.*—At noon our third storm began. At
four it was more violent than before. Now, indeed,
we could say, ' The waves of the sea were mighty,

and raged horribly. They rose up to the heavens above,' and clave 'down to hell beneath.' The winds roared round about us, and (what I never heard before) whistled as distinctly as if it had been a human voice. The ship not only rocked to and fro with the utmost violence, but shook and jarred with so unequal, grating a motion, that one could not but with great difficulty keep one's hold of anything, nor stand a moment without it. Every ten minutes came a shock against the stern or side of the ship, which one would think should dash the planks in pieces. At this time a child, privately baptized before, was brought to be received into the church. It put me in mind of Jeremiah's buying the field when the Chaldeans were on the point of destroying Jerusalem, and seemed a pledge of the mercy God designed to show us, even in the land of the living.

"We spent two or three hours after prayers in conversing suitably to the occasion, confirming one another in a calm submission to the wise, holy, gracious will of God. And now a storm did not seem so terrible as before. Blessed be the God of all consolation!

"At seven I went to the Germans. I had long before observed the great seriousness of their behaviour. Of their humility they had given a continual proof, by performing those servile offices for the other passengers, which none of the English would undertake ; for which they desired, and would receive no pay, saying, "it was good for their proud hearts," and "their loving Saviour had done more for them." And every day had given them occasion of showing a meekness, which no injury could move. If they were pushed, struck, or thrown down, they rose again and went away; but no complaint was found in their mouth. There was now an opportunity of trying whether they were delivered from the spirit of fear, as well as from that of pride, anger, and revenge. In the midst of the psalm wherewith their service began, the sea broke over, split the main-sail in pieces, covered the ship, and poured in between the decks as if the great deep had already swallowed us up. A terrible screaming began among the English. The Germans calmly sung on. I asked one of them afterwards, 'Were you not afraid?' He answered, 'I thank my God, no.' I asked, 'But were not your women and children afraid?' He replied, mildly, 'No, our women and children are not afraid to die.'

"From them I went to their crying, trembling neighbors and pointed out to them the difference in the hour of trial, between him that feareth God, and him that feareth him not. At twelve the wind fell. This was the most glorious day which I have hitherto seen.

"*Monday 26.*—We enjoyed the calm. I can conceive no difference, comparable to that between a smooth and a rough sea, except that which is between a mind calmed by the love of God, and one torn up by the storms of earthly passions.

"*Thursday 29.*—About seven in the evening, we fell in with the skirts of a hurricane. The rain as well as the wind was extremely violent. The sky was so dark in a moment that the sailors could not so much as see the ropes, or set about furling the sails. The ship must, in all probability, have overset, had not the wind fell as suddenly as it rose. Toward the end of it, we had that appearance on each of the masts, which (it is thought) the ancients called Castor and Pollux.

Joseph Schaitberger
Symbol Psalm 25. V. 21.
Schlecht und recht das behüte mich,
denn ich harre dein.

Schaitberger, the religious leader of the Salzburgers.

It was a small ball of white fire like a star. The mariners say it appears either in a storm (and then commonly upon the deck), or just at the end of it, and then it is usually on the masts or sails.

"*Friday 30.*—We had another storm, which did us no other harm than splitting the foresail. Our bed being wet, I laid me down on the floor, and slept sound till morning. And I believe I shall not find it needful to go to bed (as it is called) any more.

"*Sunday, February 1.*—We spoke with a ship of Carolina; and Wednesday 4, came within sounding. About noon, the trees were visible from the masts, and in the afternoon from the main deck. In the evening lesson were these words; "A great door, and effectual, is opened." O let no one shut it!

"*Thursday 5.*—Between two and three in the afternoon God brought us all safe into the Savannah river."

"VON RECK'S JOURNAL.[1]

1736.

"*January 31.*—A great Shower of Rain fell and the Wind changed to WEST. Thus God confounds the Opinions of Men, and convinces them that He is Almighty and Master of the Winds; for the Sailors, who had persuaded us that the Trade-Wind blew constantly from the same Quarter, found now the contrary.

"*February 6.*—At Night a tempestuous Wind arose, but God in his Goodness held his Almighty hand over

---

[1] *An Extract of the Journal of Mr. Commissary Von Reck.* Published by direction of the Society for Promoting Christian Knowledge, London, 1734. Reprinted in Force's *Historical Tracts*, Washington, 1846. Vol. IV., Nos. 5, 6, 7.

us, and was pleased the next Day to give us a good
Wind, which advanced us five or six Miles an Hour.

"*February 16.*—At Two in the Afternoon the Wind
turned contrary N. by W., but being very gentle, the
Sea was calm all that Night. It is remarkable that
hitherto the contrary Winds have always been gentle,
and immediately followed by a calm, so that we never
went back.

"*February 17.*—We had this Evening at Prayers
PSALM I, 14. OFFER UNTO GOD THANKSGIVING AND
PAY THY VOWS UNTO THE MOST HIGHEST; Which we
heartily did, for all his loving Mercies vouchsafed
unto us; and at the same time, we Vowed a Vow, as
JACOB did in GEN. 28 and the 20th Verse.

"*February 18.*—At two in the afternoon the Wind
was strong at S., and soon after it proved contrary,
and extremely violent. I was very much surprised
to see the Sea rise so high; a Tempest darkened the
Sky; the Waves swelled and foamed; and everything threatened to overwhelm us in the Deep. All
the Sails were furled; the violence of the wind was so
great that it tore the Main Sail in pieces. Besides
which, the Mate cried out that the Water rose fast in
the Hold; but though he spoke Truth, the Ship received no damage. We sighed, we cried unto God,
and prayed him to help us. He heard and comforted
us by some Passages of the Holy Scripture, as ISA.
51, 15, PSAL. 39, 7, 8, JOB chap. 14 and 17.

"*February 20.*—We saw a Scotch Ship, bound for
Charles-town, and soon lost sight of her again.

"*February 27.*—Last night we had the Wind contrary W.S.W., but God Granted us a sweet Repose
and renewed our Strength, the better to undergo a

Tempest, which a wind at W. by S. brought upon us by Break of Day. This storm was more dreadful than the other. One sees always death present in a Storm, and is more sensibly convinced of this Truth, that there may be but a moment between Life and Death. Wherefore those who are not thoroughly converted to God, and assured of the happiness of the Life to come, are the most miserable at Sea, for if they chance to perish, they perish in their sins. We made the Holy Scriptures our Refuge, some Passages whereof did mightily comfort us, as Isa. 54, 7, 8, and the following Verses, Luk. 18, 7, 8, Heb. v. 7, Mic. 7, v. 18. Divine Mercy preserved us through our Saviour, and at night the Wind abated."

The Palatine emigration of 1710 did not escape all these perils. The younger Weiser estimates the mortality on the voyage and immediately after as seventeen hundred, and his father and Scheff, in their petitions to the Board of Trade, August 2, 1720, give the same figure as that of those who " died on board, or at their landing by unavoidable sickness." But as they fix the number of emigrants as four thousand, the discrepancy in the records of the mortality is based upon the discrepancy in the record of the entire company. Governor Hunter reported immediately after his arrival: " The poor people have been mighty sickly, but recover apace. We have lost about four hundred and seventy of our number." One vessel was yet to be heard from. Two hundred and fifty are reported as having died of ship fever shortly after landing. The official report made by Mr. Du Pre to the Board of

Your Affectionate Servant
John Wesley

Trade, January 6, 1711, gives the number of survivors, when he left New York, probably in October, as 2,227. As Boehme's figures of 3,086, as the number of those who embarked, seem to be accurate, the entire loss was 859, of whom 609, or twenty per cent. of the company died on the voyage. In his petition in 1720, Scheff declares that the Palatines "lost most of their young children at their going from home to America." Boehme states that those packed in the lowest parts of the vessels were without fresh air and sunlight, and, under these circumstances, the small and tender children among them generally died. "Of some families, neither parents nor children survive." In one ship eighty died, and one hundred more were lying sick at one time. The causes assigned are two: first, the crowded condition of the vessels, and, secondly, the merciless treatment of the captains, who did not provide good and wholesome food. They landed a crushed, sick and dispirited band of exiles, after a voyage of about six months, as the vessels came in irregularly and differed in the exact time of the passage. One of them, *The Herbert*, was grounded on the coast of Long Island, July 7th, twenty-one days after the first came to shore. "The men are safe," writes Hunter, "but the goods are much damaged." The tenth vessel, *The Berkley Castle*, on July 24, was six weeks overdue; although its later start from Plymouth must be taken into account. The grounding of *The Herbert* has been made the basis for a romantic story and a beautiful poem by Whittier. Local tradition had told of a vessel called *The Palatine*, that was lured by false lights upon the rocks and then robbed and its passengers murdered. Certain graves, said to be those of Palatines, traceable in the vicinity, are referred to as evidences of the truth of the story. Governor Hunter's statement that the men were safe is interpreted as referring only to the English on board. But, as *The Herbert* according to Hunter carried all the arms and tents of the expedition, and the goods on board were reported only as much damaged, any attack upon them or any acts of piracy would have been related. Nor would he have been so indifferent to the murder of some of the Palatines, when in his despatch he speaks sympathizingly of their sickness at sea, and his mind was so intent upon plans in which he hoped to derive great gain from the industry of every colonist. They may have been wrecked by false lights; but if so the hopes of the wreckers were blasted by the force that they found that they would encounter. The poet, however, has pictured the details of the plot to its consummation:

" Old wives spinning their webs of tow,
　Or rocking weirdly to and fro
　In and out of the peat's dull glow,

" And old men mending their nets of twine,
　Talk together of dream and sign,
　Talk of the lost ship *Palatine*;

" The ship that a hundred years before,
　Freighted deep with its goodly store,
　In the gales of the equinox went ashore.

" The eager islanders one by one,
　Counted the shots of her signal gun,
　And heard the crash when she drove right on!

" Into the teeth of death she sped :
(May God forgive the hands that fed
The false lights over the rocky Head).

" O men and brothers! what sights were there!
White upturned faces, hands stretched out in prayer!
Where waves had pity, could ye not spare?

" Down swooped the wreckers, like birds of prey
Tearing the heart of the ship away,
And the dead had never a word to say.

"And then with ghastly shimmer and shine
Over the rocks and the seething brine,
They burned the wreck of the *Palatine*."

The foundation of truth in the tradition may have been
the wreck of a Palatine vessel at some later time, that in
some way was diverted from its course to Pennsylvania.
The prayers of the band whose history we have been re-
counting for protection from such perils were heard.
They had trials enough before as well as behind them to
be spared such a calamity.

CHAPTER V.—IN NEW YORK.

Seal of Province of New York.

ON landing at New York, they were sent to Nuttal's, now Governor's Island, then the quarantine station, to be nursed and recruited for still further trials. To lessen the burden of providing for them, the children fit for service were bound out, an expedient, which, however, justifiable, separated families in a time of distress, as the hand of death had already fallen heavily upon them, and practically enslaved some who in Germany had been reared in homes that had never known want.

Meanwhile Hunter proceeded to the execution of his visionary schemes that he had projected in England. His plans for accumulating extensive revenues through the services of the Palatines were as unpractical as Brad-

(110)

THE PENNSYLVANIA-GERMAN SOCIETY.

A STREET SCENE IN NEW YORK, 1709.

FROM AN OLD SKETCH.

dock's subsequent military campaigns against the Indians. The responsibility for the care of the immigrants lay upon him. When the appropriations, made upon his estimate of necessities, were exhausted, he did not hesitate to devote his private resources to the support of the people, and soon found them insufficient. The Palatines, on the other hand, finding the promises made them unfulfilled, and understanding, for the first time, the full meaning of the pledge they had made in England, regarded him as their enemy and defrauder. To add to these perplexities, the Provincial Council of New York disputed the right of the Crown to pay Hunter's salary from the income of the Province. Some sympathy must be felt for a man thus in the center of a triangular fire, especially in the extremity in which he wrote, four years later, to the Lord High Treasurer of England, that he must continue to throw himself at His Lordship's feet, until he kicked him away, and must beg for but one-fourth of the Palatines' debts to stop the mouths of clamorous creditors.

In one year, according to Hunter's reckoning, the Palatines should have been able to subsist themselves, and, after that, a prompt return was to be made for the amount that the Government had expended for their transportation and maintenance. In the autumn of 1710, some 1,500 were, therefore, taken up the Hudson to the lands of Robert Livingstone, from whom 6,000 acres were at once purchased for 266 English pounds sterling, while 800 additional acres were purchased the following spring, and 6,333 acres, on the other side of the Hudson, were also utilized. On the eastern side, three towns were laid out, the entire district being known as East Camp; while the two towns on the west side constituted West Camp. Each family was provided with a lot forty feet front and fifty feet deep. An additional village soon sprang up on each side. Large pine forests were in the immediate vicinity.

The Founding of a Home in the New World.

When all were quartered, the Lords of the Treasury received rose-colored reports from Hunter. "The great project," he wrote, "could not fail of success. 15,000 pounds a year for the next two years, would do the work effectually. Her Majesty might depend upon tar enough for her navy from her colonies forever; for there was

The Old Quassaick Church. Built during the ministration of Rev. Michael Christian Knoll.

pitch pine enough, if the number of hands was employed, to serve all Europe."

But the Board of Trade was not satisfied. Mr. Du Pre, the Commissary, was summoned before them and examined, as to why the Governor wanted subsistence for the Palatines for more than one year, as at first proposed. Then came out the stern facts "that the first year may be looked upon as lost, because of the usual hard weather prevailing there in the winter; and that, in the second year, the time would be insufficient to clear the ground and to raise enough grain for their subsistence, and in the third year, a great portion of their labor would be devoted to preparing the trees for the manufacture of tar."

The prospect became still darker when more was learned of the process of manufacture. For two years, the trees had to be treated before being available for the purpose. Finland tar, the best in the market, it was discovered, was selling for four shillings a barrel, one-half of the price upon which Governor Hunter had calculated, when estimating the money productivity of the Palatines.

But Hunter hoped against hope. He would not admit his mistake. Even in 1712, he writes most encouragingly of the progress made, and that 100,000 trees were ready to be cut for tar. His one difficulty, he complains, is that of bearing alone the heavy pecuniary responsibility imposed upon him. He had gone on, he says, laying out all the money he and his friends were masters of, for subsisting and employing that people, but had not heard that any of his bills were paid. He had reaped nothing but fatigue,

torture and trouble, and the pleasure of having surmounted
opposition and difficulties next to insurmountable. There
was no revenue to support his government, the frontiers
were exposed, and "the Indians, though but a handful,
were saucy, while the officers of the Government were all
a starving."

The man who profited by the transaction seems to have
been Livingstone. The Earl of Clarendon describes him
as "a very ill man," who had practiced extensive frauds
on the Government, and laments that Hunter has fallen

into his hands.   Reference to the commission of Capt. Kidd
printed on a preceding page (see above p. 88) shows that
the partner with Lord Bellamont in sending Kidd out as
privateer was "Robert Livingston, Esq."

The Palatines were indignant that, without consulting
them, Hunter should make with Livingstone terms, according to which they were ultimately to pay the latter.   The
great mistake of the English Government throughout, had
been, that it dealt with these people *en masse*, or as a community, and not as individuals; and, that in its measures
for their relief, instead of treating them as impoverished
freemen, it virtually enslaved them.   An assertion of their
rights was inevitable.   Not unwilling to work, and ready,
upon equitable terms, to repay all that had been expended
for them, they asked only that each individual should receive the rewards of his own toil.   Having taken the oath
of allegiance, they endeavored to conduct themselves as
loyal, law-abiding citizens, as their cheerful participation
in the expedition against Montreal in 1711 under General
Nicholson, and their subsequent response to the appeal for
the defence of Albany, when it was threatened by the
French and Indians, testify.   In the Canadian campaign,
John Conrad Weiser, Hartman Weinbecker and John Peter
Kneskern were the captains.   On each of these occasions,
the Palatines furnished three hundred soldiers.   As six
hundred was the quota of the Province of New York for
this expedition, although it was somewhat enlarged, the
Palatine contingent distributed in the regiments of Colonels
Schuyler and Ingoldsbey formed a very large proportion of

: army. If Hunter's statement of the resolution of the
.sembly of New York be correct, the Palatines were not
ated with proper respect in the action, by which the
ovince proposed at first to raise as its quota " three hun-
:d and fifty Christians, one hundred and fifty Long Island
lians, and one hundred Palatines !" While the state-
nt of the number furnished as three hundred is official
l is mentioned by the authorities several times, the rosters
.t have been preserved are incomplete. But the names
the men, who, notwithstanding the injustice under which
:y were suffering and protesting, were ready, one year
er their arrival, to respond to the call to defend their
)pted country, are worthy of preservation. Among
m are the ancestors of many Pennsylvania Germans.

"*From Queensberry:* John Conrad Weiser, Cap-
tain ; Christian Haber, Andreas Bergman, Johannis
Feeg, Mattheus Kuntz, Mattheus Reinbolt, Joh. Peter
Dopff, John Jacob Reisch, Carl Nehr, Henrich Jung,
Hen. Hoffman, Werner Deichert, George Mueller,
Fred. Bellenger, Hen. Widerwachs, Geo. Mathias,
Christo. Hagedorn, Frantz Finck, Andreas Schurtz,
Peter Hagedorn, Niclaus Weber, Wm. George, Lieut.,
Fred. Schaffer, Anth. Ichard, John Peter Sein, John
Jacob Munsinger, Johan Leyer, Jacob Kuhn, Hen.
Mathous, Nicklaus Eckard, Martin Dilleback, Niclaus
Feller, Jacob Schnell, Jacob Webber, William Nel-
les, Johannis Kisler, Geo. Breigel, Joh. Schaffer, Geo.
Dachstader, Johannes Zaysdorf.

"*From Haybury:* John Christopher Fucks, John
Wm. Daies, John Wm. Schaff, Christian Bauch, Peter
Hayd, Henr. Hammer, Mich. Ittich, Johan. Kyser,

118   *The Pennsylvania-German Society.*

Jacob Cup, Paulus Dientzer, Melch. Foltz, John
Segendorf, Philip Laux, Abraham Langen, Jno.
Jacob Schultz, Joh. Wm. Hambuch, Niclaus Laux,
Niclaus Gottel, Paulus Reitchoff.

"*From Annesburg:* Hartmann Weindecker, Captain. Joh. Wm. Dill, Peter Speis, Herman Bitzer,
Johannes Schue, John Wm. Schneider, Jacob Bast,
Johannes Blass, Johann Wm. Kammer, Joh. Bonroth,
Johannes Benhard, Sebastian Fischer, Niclaus Hayd,
Henrick Klein, Ben. Balt. Stuper, Casper Rauch,
Hans Hen. Zeller, Johannes Zeller, Samuel Kuhn,
Gerhard Schaffer, Ulrich Bruckhart, Jacob Ess,
Ferdo. Mentegen, Conrad Kuhn, Valtin Kuhn, Henrich Winter, Joh. Geo. Reiffenberg, John Wm. Linck,
Jno. Martin Netzbach, Johannes Weis, Jno. Adam
Walbourn, Jno. Henry Arendorf, Danl. Busch, Jno.
Henry Conradt, Hen. Bellinger, Johan Schneider,
Marcus Bellinger, Phil. Schaffer, Johan. Kradt,
Christ. Sittenich, Jno. Henry Schmidt, Jno. Philipl
Zerbe, Niclaus Ruhl, Adam Mic. Schmidt, Conrad
Maisinger, Thos. Ruffener, Jacob Dings, Henrick
Fehling, Joh. Jost Petry, Lud. W. Schmidt.

"*From Hunterstown:* Jno. Peter Kneskern, Captain. David Huppert, Conrad Schawerman, Henrick
Sex, Frederick Bell, Jacob Kobell, Jacob Warno,
Johannes Schulteis, Reinhard Schaffer, Johannes
Roschman, Garl Uhl, Baltz Anspach, Conrad Keller,
Jno. George Schmidt, Conrad Goldman, Geo. Bender,
Jno. Henry Uhl, Tho. Schumacher, Peter Schmidt,
Johan. Schwall, Geo. Ludwig Koch, Veil Musig,
Gro. Keschner, Chris. Hills, Rudol. Stahl.

These lists are composed entirely of residents of the vil-

lages on the east side of the Hudson. There must have
been troops also from the three villages on the west side.
But the confidence of the Governor was not won by this
service, and when the campaign was over they were dis-
armed, under the apprehension that they might turn their
arms against the province. "They have since used some
artifices," writes the Governor, "and made some false
alarms in order to induce
me to restore their arms;
but to no purpose. They
are planted where they are
covered every way." A
regiment of troops is asked
for to garrison the country
in the neighborhood of the
Palatines, to keep them to
their duty. With nothing
to encourage them in their
labor, we can readily ap-
preciate Hunter's com-

Relics of the Palatines in New York.

plaint that, except by resorting to force, it was hard to keep
them at work. When, however, he adopted a more concilia-
tory method, and offered them one-half of the proceeds,
the expedient proved successful. But the Governor was
impoverished, and was at last compelled to inform them
that, during the winter of 1712-13, they must rely upon
their own resources for support. "I had no remedy left,"
he writes, "but to intimate to that people, that they should
take measures to subsist themselves during this winter upon

SA GA YEATH QUA PIETH TON,
King of the Maquas.

FEE YEE NEEN HO GA RON,
Emperor of the Six Nations.

the lands where they were planted, and such as could not, might find it by working with the inhabitants, leaving with the commissaries their names and the names of the places or landlords where they are employed during that time, that they may be in readiness upon the first public notice, given, to return to work."

Thus the contract was broken on the side of the Governor. The tidings struck consternation into the Palatines. Winter was just at hand. Starvation was imminent. Something had to be done at once, or they were lost. Thrown upon their own resources, the more enterprising among them proceeded to provide for themselves in a way Hunter had not anticipated. True to the German instinct to go to first sources, they determined, without the intervention of any third party, like Livingstone, to deal directly with the first proprietors of the soil, the Indians. They recalled the fact that several Indian chiefs, who had visited England, while they were encamped in London, had presented Queen Anne with a tract of ground, near Schoharie, for their use. A delegation headed by the elder Weiser was sent accordingly to the Indians to state their extremity, and to ask permission for them to settle on the lands that had been donated. The Indians acted in good faith. In less than two weeks after the return of the delegation, fifty families moved to Schoharie, by way of Schenectady, constructing over a portion of the way fifteen miles of roadway through the forests. Reaching their destination they found a prohibition from the Governor awaiting them, accompanied with the threat that, unless

ECON OH KOAN,
King of the River Nation.

HO NEE YEATH TAN NO RON,
King of the Generechgarich.

they would return they would be treated as rebels. No
alternative was in their power but to remain and take the
consequences. In March, 1713, they were followed by
a large number of their kindred, who broke their way
through three feet of snow. More ground was needed
for their support than the Indians had donated. Certain
citizens of Albany prompted by their antipathy towards
Germans, cherished at the time by the Dutch settlers and
their descendants, sought to preëmpt the land; but, favored
by the friendship of the Indians, all that they needed was
procured for three hundred dollars. From the Indians
they learned the use of certain roots (probably potatoes)
and wild herbs (as beans, etc.), and where to look for
them. They refer to the fact that what was said to Adam
in wrath: "Of the grass of the field thou shalt eat," was
said to them in grace.

To the Board of Trade, Hunter explained that he had
been powerless to prevent this movement. He consoled
himself with the assurance, that, while, without his license,
they could obtain no title to the land, they would prove, if
successful, a good protection for the frontier, and a new
field would be opened for the manufacture of tar.

It was to a beautiful and fertile country that they were
thus strangely led. Twenty thousand acres came into their
possession. The people, numbering from five to seven
hundred, were settled in seven villages, named after the
deputies who had treated with the Indians, and who had
then led the colony to Schoharie, viz., Kneskerndorf,
Gerlachsdorf, Fuchsendorf, Schmidtsdorf, Weisersdorf,

Hartmansdorf and Ober Weisersdorf. Four children, William Bouck, Catharine Mattice, Elizabeth Sawyer and John Earhart were born the week after their arrival. They were without a pastor, but a tailor wrote to Boehme that he was acting as a lay preacher.

Upon the history of Schoharie, whose details have been well preserved, both in contemporary documents, and by industrious collectors of traditions many years ago, we cannot linger. When we consider that the Palatines carried with them none of the agricultural implements with which they had been furnished on the Hudson; that, in the beginning, there was not even a wheelbarrow in the colony, much less a horse or a cow, the progress made with the most primitive appliances for tilling the soil was most surprising. A vivid picture of the hardships of their primitive mode of life has been drawn by a local authority: "For several years they had most of their grain floured at Schenectady. They usually went in parties of fifteen or twenty at a time, to be able to defend themselves against the wild beasts. Often there were as many women as men on these journeys, and as they had to encamp in the woods at least one night, the women frequently displayed, when in danger, as much courage as their liege lords. A skipple was the quantity usually borne by each individual, but the stronger often carried more. Not infrequently they left Schoharie to go to mill on the morning of one day, and were at home on the morning of the next; performing a journey of between forty and fifty miles in twenty-four hours or less, bearing the ordinary burden; but at such

WILLIAM C. BOUCK,

B. 1786; D. 1859.

GOVERNOR OF NEW YORK, 1843-45, NAMESAKE AND DESCENDANT OF WILLIAM BOUCK,
WHO WAS BORN DURING THE FIRST WEEK OF THE SCHOHARIE SETTLEMENT.

times, they traveled most of the night without encamping."[1]

The Palatines owed much to the continued friendly relations of the Indians. One proof is given in the fact that, during the first winter, John Conrad Weiser sent his son Conrad to live among the Mohawks and learn their language. But while the Indians were conciliated, their Dutch neighbors seemed to them merciless. Looking back, as we may now do, we must concede that there were faults on both sides. Our ancestors and kinsmen in their ignorance of the processes of law, and with a deep sense of injustice, undoubtedly forfeited some of their rights, but could not be persuaded that they were wrong. They claimed the absolute right to lands which the Indians had given or sold them, and first ignored, and then resisted every attempt of the Provincial authorities to establish the titles. When Nicholas Bayard was sent to give them deeds in the name of the Crown, upon the simple condition that each householder show the boundaries of the lands that he had taken, he was driven off under a hot fire of bullets. From Schoharie, he offered a deed to every one who would bring in payment a single ear of corn; but this offer no one accepted. In November, 1714, therefore, the lands were sold to certain Dutch citizens of Albany. The Palatines found that attempts were made to turn the Indians against them. But this was recognized as a very dangerous expedient, since Weiser's influence with the Mohawks could not be overcome. Every effort made by the

---

[1] *History of Schoharie County and Border Wars of New York*, by J. W. Simms, Albany, 1845.

purchasers to settle on the lands was resisted. An interesting report is that of Adam Vrooman to the Governor concerning the ground that he had sowed with grain, upon which the Palatines drove their horses by night; and the house that he had well under way, which he found one morning razed to the ground, the Palatines concealing their operations by driving horses with bells upon them all through the night. "John Conrad Weiser," he continues, "has been the ringleader of all factions; for he has had his son sometime to live among the Indians, and now he is turned their interpreter; so that this Weiser and his son talk with the Indians very often, and have made treaties for them, and have been busy to buy land at many places."[1] The charge was afterwards made by Hunter in Weiser's presence, before the Board of Trade in England, that he had brought down the Indians of The Five Nations upon the Dutch grantees.

Sheriff Adams was finally sent down from Albany to assert the supremacy of the law, and arrest Weiser. When he reached Weisersdorf, now Middleburg, Schoharie Co., the Palatine women took the responsibility of a defence from the shoulders of their husbands and fathers, and, under the leadership of Margeret Zeh, knocked him down, rolled him in the mud, and lifting him on a rail, carried him the distance of six or seven miles, and left him on a log bridge on the road to Albany. He returned a thoroughly bruised and humiliated man, with two broken ribs, and the loss of an eye. We must commend the for-

[1] *Documentary History of New York*, III., 412.

bearance of the Governor, in attempting no immediate arrests for this flagrant violation of the law. But unsuspecting members of the settlements who went to Albany on business, were arrested and imprisoned. That Weiser came to intimidate the Governor, with three or four hundred armed men, we know only from Hunter's testimony in Weiser's presence in 1720. In order to end the struggle, the Governor finally summoned their representatives to Albany in 1717, and informed them that, unless they purchased the ground they would be transported to another place, and their improvements paid for at an appraised value by the Province.

There seemed to be but one remedy; and that was to appeal to the Board of Trade through personal representatives. On this errand, Weiser, Scheff and Walrath were secretly sent in 1718. Captured by pirates in Delaware Bay, they were robbed, and Weiser thrice tied up and cruelly beaten. After a long delay reaching England, Pastor Boehme's influence at length secured for them a hearing before the Board ; but not until they had been imprisoned for debt, and Walrath had started for home and died. The following is the petition of Scheff and Weiser :

"That, in the year 1709, the Palatines and other Germans, being invited to come into England about four thousand of them were sent to New York in America, of whom about 1700 died on board, or at their landing in that Province by unavoidable sickness.

"That before they went on board they were promised, those remaining alive should have forty acres of land and five pounds sterling a head, besides clothes,

tools, utensils and other necessaries to husbandry to
be given on their arrival in America.

" That on their landing they were quartered in tents,
and divided into six companies, having each a captain
of their own nation, with a promise of an allowance
of fifteen pounds per annum to each commander.

" That afterwards they were removed on lands belonging to Mr. Livingstone, where they erected small
houses for shelter during the winter seasons.

" That in the Spring following they were ordered
into the woods to make pitch and tar, where they lived
about two years ; but the country not being fit to raise
any considerable quantity of naval stores, they were
commanded to build, to clear and improve the ground
belonging to a private person.

" That the Indians having yielded to Her late Majesty of pious memory a small tract of land called
Schorie for the use of the Palatines, they, in fifteen
days, cleared a way of fifteen miles through the
woods, and settled fifty families therein.

" That in the following Spring the remainder of the
said Palatines joined the said fifty families so settled
therein Schorie.

" But that country being too small for their in creas-
ing families, they were constrained to purchase some
neighboring land of the Indians, for which they were
to give three hundred pieces of eight.

" And having built small houses and huts, there
about one year after the said purchase some gentlemen
of Albany, declared to the Palatines, that themselves
having purchased the said country of Schorie of the
Governor of New York, they would not permit them
to live there, unless an agreement was also made with

those of Albany ; but that the Palatines having refused
to enter into such agreement, a sheriff and some officers were sent from Albany to seize one of their captains, who being upon his guard, the Indians were
animated against the Palatines ; but these found means
to appease the savages by giving them what they
would of their own substance.

"That in the year 1717 the Governor of New York
having summoned the Palatines to appear at Albany,
some of them being deputed went accordingly, where
they were told that unless they did agree with the
gentlemen of Albany, the Governor expected an order
from England to transport them to another place, and
that he would send twelve men to view their works
and improvements to appraise the same, and then to
give them the value thereof in money.

"But this not being done, the Palatines, to the
number of about three thousand, have continued to
manure and sow the land, that they might not be
starved for want of corn and food.

"For which manuring the gentlemen of Albany
have put in prison one man and one woman, and will
not release them, unless they have sufficient security of
One Hundred Crowns for the former.

"Now in order that the Palatines may be preserved
in the Land of Schorie, which they have purchased
of the Indians, or that they may be so settled in an
adjoining tract of land, as to raise a necessary subsistence for themselves and their families, they have
sent into England three persons, one of whom is since
dead, humbly to lay their case before His Majesty, not
doubting but that in consideration of the hardships
they have suffered for want of a secure settlement,

His Majesty's ministers and Councils will compassionate those His faithful subjects.

" Who, in the first year after their arrival willingly and cheerfully sent three hundred men to the expedition against Canada, and afterwards to the assistance of Albany which was threatened by the French and Indians, for which service they never received one penny, tho' they were upon the establishment of New York or New Jersey ; nor had they received one penny of the five pounds per head promised at their going on board from England; neither have their commanders received anything of the allowance of fifteen pounds per annum; and though the arms they had given them at the Canada expedition, which were, by special order of Her late Majesty, to be left in their possession, have been taken from them, yet they are still ready to fight against all the enemies of His Majesty and those countries, whenever there shall be occasion to show their hearty endeavor for the prosperity of their generous benefactors in England, as well as in America.

" Therefore, they hope from the justice of the Right Honorable Lords Commissioners of Trade and Plantations, to whom their petition to their excellencies the Lord Justices has been referred, that they shall be so supported by their Lordships' report, as to be represented fit objects to be secured in the land they now do inhabit, or in some near adjoining lands remaining in the right of the Crown in the said Province of New York."[1]   August 2, 1720.

But a new difficulty arose.   The far-seeing eye of Weiser had Pennsylvania in view as the proper home of his

[1] *Documents relating to the Colonial History of New York*, V., 553-5.

THE VALLEY OF SCHOHARIE.

:ople. He conceived the scheme of securing from the ,vernment an exchange of their lands in New York for hers on the Swatara. To this Scheff was violently op->sed, and accordingly filed his protest with the Board, :claring any such proposition of Weiser a violation of structions. " Your petitioner," he writes, "hearing with 'ief that John Conrad Weiser has petitioned your Lord-ips, for obtaining a tract of land called Chettery [Swa-ra], most humbly entreats your Lordships to dismiss the id Weiser's petition as being directly contrary to our structions and the inclinations of our people, who ear-:stly desire to lead a quiet and peaceable life, and are terly averse to expose their tender children and child-:aring women to another transportation by water, as still membering the loss of most of their young children at eir going from home to America." [1]

Hunter's recall to England and his appearance before e Board was an effectual obstacle to any efforts for the :nfirmation of their titles to their lands. Lands in other calities in New York were offered instead to those willing remove. Some, accepting this offer, removed to the dis-:ct known as Stony Arabia. Others, who, by their thrift, ld accumulated means, purchased their old homes. But .ll others, chiefly from Hartmansdorf and Weisersdorf fol-wed Weiser's advice, as the best solution of the problem, ld turned their faces southward towards Pennsylvania.

As we turn from New York to descend the Susquehanna ith these pioneers, we may interrupt the narrative for a

[1] *Documents relating to the Colonial History of New York*, V., 575.

few moments, and, going forward nearly a quarter of a century, look upon the closing scene of the life of their leader, as it shows whence his intrepid courage and undaunted perseverance came.

"In the year 1746," writes Henry Melchior Muhlenberg, "my wife's grandfather, Conrad Weiser, Sr., came to my house, having been living in the Province of New York, since 1710, and more recently on the borders of New England. * * * He was so much exhausted by the long and fatiguing journey at his great age, that he was almost dead when he was brought into my house. After he had been resting in bed for twenty-four hours, and had partaken of some nourishment he was refreshed. Then he began in half broken accents, devoutly to repeat the hymn : '*Schwing dich auf zu deinem Gott*,' etc., especially repeating the third verse. His eyesight was very dim ; his hearing was so dull that I could not speak much with him ; but as I listened to him repeating from his heart passages of Scripture, such as : 'Surely He hath borne our griefs,' etc., 'This is a faithful saying and worthy of all acceptation,' etc., 'God was in Christ reconciling the world unto Himself,' etc., 'For God so loved the world,' etc., I could not refrain from tears of joy. To these he added verses concerning the personal appropriation of Christ, as 'Come unto me all ye that labor,' etc., 'Him that cometh unto me I will in no wise cast out,' etc., 'Father, I have sinned against Heaven,' etc., and 'God, be merciful to me a sinner.' He repeated also '*Ach vater deck all meine Suende*,' the sixth stanza of the hymn, '*Wer weiss wie nahe mir mein Ende*.'

' O Father, cover all my sins
    With Jesus' merits, Who alone
The pardon that I covet wins,
    And make His long-sought rest my own.
My God, for Jesus' sake I pray,
Thy peace may bless my dying day.''[1]

" I had everything quieted around him, so that he might not notice the presence of any one, in order that he might alone and in spirit hold communion with the Omipresent God. * * * * He expressed an anxious desire for the Holy Supper, adding that as there had been no pastors in the region where he had been living he had not received it for some years. It was Sunday, and some members of our congregation had called before the hour of worship. So he made confession of his sins, humbled himself in the presence of his Saviour, as a poor worm, worthy of condemnation, implored grace and pardon, and asked for the Holy Spirit, that he might lead a better life. Such an impression was made on all present that they were melted to tears. * * * * In the meantime my father-in-law sent a wagon for him, furnished with a bed, and so had him conveyed to his own home, fifty miles up the country. Upon leaving, he gave us his blessing. He arrived at the house of his son, after a very fatiguing journey, and lived yet for a short time with his Joseph in Goshen. Then, at last, he fell asleep amid the loving prayers and sighs of his children and his childrens' children, who stood around him, his wandering in his pilgrimage having been continued between eighty and ninety years." [2]

---

[1] Translation of Miss Winkworth.

[2] *Hallesche Nachrichten*, old ed., pp. 161–3 ; *Lutheran Church Review*, XI., 391-4.

CHAPTER VI.—TO PENNSYLVANIA.

Arms of Pennsylvania from contemporary print.

IN 1723 under the guidance of the Indians a road was cut from the Schoharie to the Susquehanna. Over this thirty-three families transported their goods. Canoes and rafts were built, and the most of the people were thus carried to their new home, while the cattle were driven along the bank. Down the Susquehanna they went to the mouth of the Swatara, up the Swatara, to the Tulpehocken, and thence settlements were formed along that creek. Thus they become pioneers of portions of Dauphin, Lebanon and Berks counties. A tradition current in the Schoharie settlement, which may be given for what it is worth, states that twelve of the horses of the Tulpehocken colony not approving the

(134)

change, broke loose, twelve of them arriving in good condition at Schoharie a year and a half after their removal,
having·completed a journey of over three hundred miles!
A partial list of the Schoharie immigrants to the Tulpehocken region has been included by Mr. Rupp in Appendix XIV. of his invaluable book. Five years later, they
were followed by others. The younger Weiser states that
the settlement was made in Pennsylvania without the consent of the Proprietary of Pennsylvania or his commission-
aries, and against the consent of the Indians. For a considerable time, they were absolutely without any law or
government. The older Weiser did not accompany the expedition he had projected; the younger removed to Tulpehocken from Schoharie in 1729. The preceding year,
fifteen heads of families had petitioned for the right of
purchasing land, stating that fifty other families were in
the same circumstances, and desired the same privilege.[1]

Meanwhile during all these years the emigration to Pennsylvania had proceeded, notwithstanding the diversion to
the Carolinas and New York. The cruel diversion of a
large number of Germans to Louisiana in 1716 in connection with the so-called Mississippi bubble of John Law
and the death of the vast majority was an episode that only
made Pennsylvania more popular. The Palatines spread
‑the story of their wrongs far and wide among their kinsmen in Germany, and turned the tide whither it had been
first directed by the efforts and invitations of Penn. Peter
Kalm, the Swedish naturalist, who visited this country in

[1] *Colonial Records of Pennsylvania*, III., p. 323.

En
Resa
Til
Norra AMERICA,

På
Kongl. Swenska Wetenskaps
Academiens befallning,
Och
Publici kostnad,
förrättad
Af

PEHR KALM,

Oeconomiæ Profeſſor i Åbo, ſamt Ledamot af
Kongl. Swenſka Wetenſkaps-Academien.

Tom. II.

Med Kongl. Maj:ts Allernådigſte Privilegio.

STOCKHOLM,
Tryckt på LARS SALVII koſtnad, 1756.

Title of Kalm's *Travels in North America.*

1748, writes: "The Germans wrote to their relatives and friends, and advised them, if ever they intended to come to America, not to go to New York, where the Government had shown itself to be inequitable. This advice had so much influence that the Germans who afterwards went in great numbers to North America, constantly avoided New York, and always went to Pennsylvania. It sometimes happened that they were forced to go on board such ships as were bound for New York, but they were scarcely got on shore, before they hastened to Pennsylvania, in sight of all the inhabitants of New York."[1]

The efforts of Kocherthal had only temporarily diverted or retarded the main stream of German emigration to Pennsylvania. It now flowed on in a strong and steady current, gathering around the nucleus formed by the Frankford Land Company, thence diffusing itself throughout the southeastern corner of the province, and after crossing the Susquehanna, sending its overflow into Maryland and the Shenandoah Valley of Virginia. The details of this immigration are outside the limits of the present paper, which, according to the assignment, is simply to bring the emigrants to our borders, and leave them there, for other writers to complete the work. A few facts, however, are in place.

Pennsylvania, we believe, became a favorite of German emigrants because of the religious principles embodied in its laws. These were, first the clear recognition of Christianity as the basis of the government, and, secondly, the

[1] *Travels in America*, I., p. 270 sq.

toleration granted, within certain limits for various forms
of Christianity. The fact that the German emigration
proceeded in clearly-marked waves, according to diverse
denominations and sects, beginning with those most persecuted in Europe, and thence proceeding to those where the
religious restraints in the mother country were more a
matter of annoyance than of persecution, supports this
opinion. "The History of Religious Liberty in Pennsylvania" would be a fruitful theme for an entire paper.

Penn, in the preface to his *Frame of Laws*, bases all
civil government upon Divine authority as proclaimed in
the Holy Scriptures, and lays down principles in axiomatic
form that are worthy of lasting memory. "Let men be
good, and the government cannot be bad; if it be ill,
they will cure it. But if men be bad, let the government
be never so good, they will endeavor to warp and spoil it
to their turn." The very first law contained in the Petition
of Rights of 1682 makes it one of the qualifications of
members of the Assembly and of those who have the
right to vote for members, that they "shall be such as
profess and declare that they believe in Jesus Christ to be
the Son of God, the Saviour of the world."[1] Among the
laws agreed upon in England in 1682, and in force in
1682–1700, is the following: "That all persons living in
this province, who confess and acknowledge the One Almighty and Eternal God to be the Creator, Upholder and
Ruler of the world, and that hold themselves obliged in
conscience to live peaceably and justly in civil society,

[1] *Duke of York's Laws*, etc., Harrisburg, 1879, p. 19 sq.

shall in no ways be molested or prejudiced for their religious persuasion or practice in matters of faith and worship, nor shall they be compelled at any time to frequent or maintain any religious worship, place or ministry whatever."[1] In 1697, this law was reënacted, with the additional clause: "and if any person shall abuse or deride any other for his or her different persuasion or practice in matter of religion, such person shall be looked upon as a disturber of the peace and be punished accordingly." This was afterwards declared by enactment to be the very first of the Fundamental Laws of the Province.[2] When again enacted in 1700, it was repealed by the Queen in Council upon the exception of the Attorney-General—"I am of the opinion that this law is not fit to be confirmed, no regard being had in it to the Christian religion, and also for that in the indulgence allowed to the Quakers in England, by the statute of the first by William and Mary, chapt. 18 (which sort of people are also the principal inhabitants of Pennsylvania) they are obliged by the declaration to profess faith in God, and in Jesus Christ, His Eternal Son, the True God, and in the Holy Spirit, One God Blessed forevermore; and to acknowledge the Scriptures of the Old and New Testaments to be given by Divine inspiration, and also for that none can tell for what conscientious practices allowed by this act may extend to."[3]

In accordance, therefore, with these exceptions of the Attorney-General, there resulted the Act of 1705-6, which

---

[1] *Duke of York's Laws*, etc., p. 102 sq.   [2] Ib., p. 154.

[3] *Statutes at Large for Pennsylvania*, 1682-1800. Compiled by James F. Mitchell and Henry Flanders, II., 489.

was in force during the entire period embraced in this paper. The recognition of the Trinity and of the inspiration of the Holy Scriptures was in no way objectionable to the great body of the German immigrants, while the liberty offered from the restraints of ecclesiasticism was particularly appreciated not merely by those who were generally regarded as "sects," but by the adherents also of the Pietistic movement. The Act is as follows:

> "Almighty God, being only Lord of conscience, author of all divine knowledge, faith and worship, who can only enlighten the minds and convince the understanding of people; in due reverence to His sovereignty over the souls of mankind, and the better to unite the Queen's subjects in interest and affection; Be it enacted, that no person now or at any time hereafter dwelling or residing within this province, who shall profess faith in God the Father, and in Jesus Christ His only Son, and in the Holy Spirit, One God blessed forevermore, and shall acknowledge the Holy Scriptures of the Old and New Testaments to be given by divine inspiration, and when lawfully required shall profess and declare that they will live peaceably under the constituted government, shall, in any case, be molested or prejudiced for his or her conscience persuasion, nor shall he or she be at any time compelled to frequent or maintain any religious worship, place or ministry whatever, contrary to his or her mind, but shall freely and fully enjoy his or her Christian liberty in all respects, without molestation or interruption."[1]

---

[1] Acts of the General Assembly of Pennsylvania at session October 14, 1705–February 12, 1706. *Laws of the Commonwealth of Pennsylvania*, 1700–1810, I, p. 94.

Among the movements which may be ascribed to these laws guaranteeing liberty of conscience, was the Mennonite emigration to the Pequea District in Lancaster County, between 1709 and 1717—a branch from the Germantown settlement forming the beginning, which was greatly reinforced by recruits from Switzerland and Germany secured through the mission to Europe of Martin Kendig. Dunkards and other Mennonites are said to have reached Lehigh County not much later. Even before this (1704–12), before and contemporaneously with the Palatine emigration to New York, other of their countrymen, mostly Reformed and Lutheran, can be traced filling up the Oley region, with its center in Berks, although standing in the old records for a much more extensive territory than the township of that name. So also the District in Montgomery County about the headwaters of the Perkiomen was settled by the same people before the Palatines descended the Susquehanna. The Allens and Wisters and other land speculators in Philadelphia had found customers among those who arrived at the port, and had sold them homes in Northampton. The Palatines from New York at Tulpehocken and Quitapahilla had attracted to this country many of their relatives and friends whom they had left in Germany.

No more vivid picture could be drawn of the condition of the majority of the emigrants than a letter of Casper Wistar, already referred to. We quote from the " *Sammlung auserlesener Materien zum Bau des Reichs Gottes* " (Leipzig), for 1733, where it is credited to the Leipzig

" *Zeitungen* " of May 22, 1733, having been written in Philadelphia, November 8, 1732.

" Being importuned daily by so many of our countrymen to relieve them from the great distress, into which they have come, partially through their own thoughtlessness, and partially by the persuasion of others, and it being absolutely impossible to help all, sympathy for the poor people still in the Fatherland, and who, before undertaking such a journey, have time to reflect, constrains me to give a true account of the condition of things in this new land. I make this particular request that these facts may be reported everywhere, that no one may have the excuse for learning them only from his own personal experience.

" Some years ago this was a very fruitful country, and, like all new countries, but sparsely inhabited. Since the wilderness required much labor, and the inhabitants were few, ships that arrived with German emigrants were cordially welcomed. They were immediately discharged, and by their labor very easily earned enough to buy some land. Pennsylvania is but a small part of America, and has been open now for some years, so that not only many thousand Germans, but English and Irish have settled there, and filled all parts of the country; so that all who now seek land must go far into the wilderness, and purchase it at a higher price.

" Many hardships also are experienced on the voyage. Last year one of the ships was driven about the ocean for twenty-four weeks, and of its one hundred and fifty passengers, more than one hundred starved to death. To satisfy their hunger, they caught mice and rats ; and a mouse brought half a gulden. When the survivors at last reached land, their sufferings were aggravated by their arrest, and the exaction from them of the entire fare for both living and dead. This year ten ships with three thousand souls have arrived.

" One of these vessels was seventeen weeks on the way and about sixty of its passengers died at sea. All the survivors are sick and feeble, and, what is worst, poor and without means ; hence, in a community like this where money is scarce, they are a burden, and every day there are deaths among them. Every person over fourteen years old, must pay six doubloons (about 90 dollars) passage from Rotterdam, and those between four and fourteen must pay half that amount. When one is without the money, his only resource is to sell himself for a term of from three to eight years or more, and to serve as a slave. Nothing but a poor suit of clothes is received when his time has expired. Families endure a great trial when they see the father purchased by one master, the mother by another, and each of the children by another. All this for the money only that they owe the Captain. And yet they are only too glad, when after waiting long, they at last find some one willing to buy them ; for the money of the country is well nigh exhausted. In view of these circumstances, and the tedious, expensive and perilous voyage, you should not advise any one for whom you wish well to come hither. All I can say is that those who think of coming should weigh well what has been above stated, and should count the cost, and, above all, should go to God for counsel and inquire whether it be His will, lest they may undertake that whereof they will afterward repent. If ready to hazard their lives and to endure patiently all the trials of the voyage, they must farther think whether over and above the cost they will have enough to purchase cattle, and to provide for other necessities. No one should rely upon friends whom he may have here; for they have enough to do, and many a one reckons in this without his host. Young and able-bodied persons, who can do efficient work, can, nevertheless, always find some one who will purchase them for two, three or four years; but they must be unmarried. For young married persons, particularly when the wife is with child, no one cares to have. So also with old people and children. Of mechanics there are a considerable number already here; but a good mechanic who can bring with him sufficient capital to avoid beginning with debt, may do well, although of almost all classes and occupations, there are already more than too many. All this I have, out of sincere love for the interests of my neighbor, deemed it necessary to communicate concerning the present condition in Pennsylvania. With this I commit my beloved friend to the protection of God, and always remain

" His sincere friend,

" CASPAR WISTAR."

But it is a mistake to suppose that these emigrants were always impoverished. They often brought with them a modest capital with which to begin life on this side of the ocean. Some were in good circumstances and were able to buy large farms. Their usual course was from Germany to Rotterdam in Holland, thence to England, and thence to Philadelphia. " The frequency with which the same craft, as shown by the records, entered the capes of the Delaware, implied a traffic partaking somewhat of the character of a ferry. For year after year the ships *St. Andrew, Phœnix, Dragon, Patience, Morto*n use, *Pennsylvania, The Two Brothers, Nancy* and many others discharged their human cargoes at Philadelphia, the average passenger lists embracing one hundred and fifty souls. In the year 1719 some six thousand are said to have landed, in 1732 ten vessels with three thousand passengers, and Proud avers that in the year 1749 twelve thousand Germans arrived in the Province. Sypher claims that prior to 1727 fifty thousand people, mostly from the Rhine country, had emigrated to the Quaker colony."[1] At the middle of the century the German population of Pennsylvania was about one-half of the whole. Not until 1717 was any record of passengers kept, but as the stream began to flow in large mass the wise precaution of Lieut.-Governor Keith, requiring all immigrants to take the oath of allegiance and be registered in Philadelphia, furnished the historical data which the late Mr. I. D. Rupp has industriously gathered and embodied in his valuable Thirty Thousand Names. These lists of male immigrants over sixteen years of age began in 1727. It is possible they are incomplete, as there are gaps that may, and yet may not be explained, since these vessels all arrived at the same period of the year. Thus there are no records between October, 1727, and August, 1728; September, 1728, and August,

---

[1] A. D. Melick, Jr., *The Pennsylvania Magazine of History and Biography*, X., 391.

1729, September, 1729, and August, 1730. In the last three weeks of 1732 no less than 1,500 people arrived, while in August and September, 1733, 1,369 are reported. The Lutheran pastors, Muhlenberg, Brunnholtz and Handschuh, in reporting the religious condition of the German immigrants to Halle, in 1754, divide the history of the immigration into five periods. The first was from 1680 to 1708; the second, from 1708 to 1720. Of the latter, they say: "In the years 1708, 1709, 1710 to 1720, when there was a great movement from the Palatinate to England, and a large number of people were sent thence to New York, under Queen Anne, not a few came from the same source to Pennsylvania also." They were largely people of a religious character, and brought with them Arndt's *True Christianity* and volumes of sermons and Prayer Books, besides the ponderous Bibles so familiar to their descendants among the heirlooms of their fathers; but, according to this report, their neglect to provide for themselves churches and ministers bore bitter fruit in the relative religious indifference of the next generation. Towards the close of the same period, they note the arrival of members of such communities as the Tunkers, Mennonites, Schwenckfelders, etc., of whom we have more accurate information elsewhere. The third period is from 1720 to 1730, with a large immigration from the Palatinate, Würtemberg, Hesse-Darmstadt and other districts, as well as of many of the New York Palatines. Among them, there seemed more religious earnestness; but their extreme poverty prevented them from securing sufficient pastors. At the close of this period and the beginning of the next, from 1730 to 1740, a still more extensive immigration followed. This immigration moved in successive waves, representing different religious denominations.

Peter Tranberg
Pastor in Willmington

Henry Melchior Muhlenberg
minister at Providence and New Hanover.

Gabr. Naaman Minister
at ye Swede Church at Uicaco.

Peter Brunin holtz,
minister at Philadelphia
(and) Germantown.

Signatures of the German Lutheran pastors, Muhlenberg and Brunnholtz, with those of their Swedish associates at Wilmington, and Gloria Dei Church, Philadelphia.

With some marked exceptions, it may be said that the communities composed of separatists from the State Churches came first; then came the Reformed; then the Lutherans; then the Moravians. The Reformed pastor Weiss reports in 1731 no less than 15,000 members of his Church in Pennsylvania. Twenty years later Rev. Michael Schlatter estimated the entire population as 190,000, of whom 90,000 were Germans and 30,000 Reformed. Dr. J. H. Dubbs claims that up to the middle of the last century, the Reformed were by far the most numerous religious body in the Province. The Reformed Classis of Amsterdam in 1751, wrote that Pennsylvania was probably a Pella or Zoar, whence the godly might escape from the calamities threatening the Old World, and add that thousands of immigrants, chiefly from the Palatinate and Switzerland, and the majority of them adherents to the Reformed faith, have already taken refuge there.[1]

Welcomed at first, and their labor in advancing the general prosperity recognized, the extent of the immigration began as early as 1717 to occasion apprehension on the part of the English settlers, which increased to positive hostility, as years brought no cessation of the stream. In 1728, Governor Thomas estimated the Germans as constituting three-fifths of the entire population. The words of Benjamin Franklin in 1751 may be recalled as a proof of the vastness of the movement: "Why should the Palatine boors be suffered to swarm into our settlements, and, by herding together, establish their language and manners, to

---

[1] Fresenius, *Pastoral-Sammlung*, XII., 219.

the exclusion of ours? Why should Pennsylvania, founded by the English, become a colony of aliens, who will shortly be so numerous as to Germanize us, instead of our Anglicifying them, and will never adopt our language or customs any more than they can acquire our complexion?" Dr. William Smith, the Provost of the University of Pennsylvania, thought it possible that the Provincial Legislature would be forced to appoint an official interpreter, that one-half of the legislators might be able to understand the other half, and to save Pennsylvania from the threatened heathenism, organized a *"Society for the Propagation of the Gospel among the Germans!"* Alarmists were constantly raising the cry of an imminent peril of an alliance between the Pennsylvania Germans and the French, on the west, that would be fatal to English dominance. Franklin was soon made to feel that he had committed a political blunder by his strongly expressed hostility to the immigrants, and tried to explain that the term "boor," he had employed, was only a synonym for "farmer;" while he freely conceded the important contribution they made to the development of Pennsylvania. "Their industry and frugality are exemplary. They are excellent husbandmen and contribute greatly to the improvement of a country." In 1738, the Governor, in a message to the Provincial Assembly, had declared: "This Province has been for some time the asylum of the distressed Protestants of the Palatinate, and other parts of Germany; and I believe it may with truth be said that the present flourishing condition of it is in great measure owing to the industry of those people." [1]

When in 1729, Thomas Mackin, the Principal of the Philadelphia Academy, undertook to celebrate the growing prosperity of the Province, he both alludes to the numbers and the importance of our fathers in the words :

> " Twas hither first the British crossed the main;
> Thence many others left their native plain;
> Hibernia's sons forsake their native home;
> And from Germania, crowded vessels come.
> Not for themselves alone the British care;
> Since every stranger may partake a share.
> Hence still more culture shall the soil receive,
> And every year increasing plenty give.
> Cleared from the woods more fruitful land they gain,
> And yellow Ceres fills the extended plain.
> Here bubbling fountains flow through every mede,
> Where flocks and herds delight to drink and feed.
> The marshy grounds improved rich meadows yield,
> The wilderness is made into a field."

[1] Colonial Records, IV., 312.

Other books by the author:

Amana: William Rufus Perkins' and Barthinius L. Wick's History of the Amana Society, or Community of True Inspiration

Americana Germanica: Paul Ben Baginsky's Bibliography of German Works Relating to America, 1493-1800

Biography of Baron Von Steuben, the Army of the American Revolution and Its Organizer: Rudolf Cronau's Biography of Baron von Steuben

CD: German-American Biographical Index (Midwest Families)

CD: Germans, Volume 2

CD: The German Colonial Era (four volumes)

Cincinnati's German Heritage

Covington's German Heritage

Custer: Frederick Whittaker's Complete Life of General George A. Custer, Major General of Volunteers, Brevet Major General U.S. Army and Lieutenant-Colonel Seventh U.S. Cavalry

Dayton's German Heritage: Karl Karstaedt's Golden Jubilee History of the German Pioneer Society of Dayton, Ohio

Early German-American Newspapers: Daniel Miller's History

German Americans in the Revolution

German Immigration to America: The First Wave

German Pioneer Life and Domestic Customs

German Pioneer Lifestyle

German Pioneers in Early California: Erwin G. Gudde's History

German-American Achievements: 400 Years of Contributions to America

German-Americana: A Bibliography

Germany and America, 1450-1700

Kentucky's German Pioneers: H.A. Rattermann's History

Lives and Exploits of the Daring Frank and Jesse James: Thaddeus Thorndike's Graphic and Realistic Description of Their Many Deeds of Unparalleled Daring in the Robbing of Banks and Railroad Trains

Louisiana's German Heritage: Louis Voss' Introductory History

Maryland's German Heritage: Daniel Wunderlich Nead's History

Memories of the Battle of New Ulm: Personal Accounts of the Sioux Uprising. L. A. Fritsche's History of Brown County, Minnesota (1916)

Michigan's German Heritage: John Andrew Russell's History of the German Influence in the Making of Michigan

Ohio's German Heritage

Outbreak and Massacre by the Dakota Indians in Minnesota in 1862: Marion P. Satterlee's Minute Account of the Outbreak, with Exact Locations, Names of All Victims, Prisoners at Camp Release, Refugees at Fort Ridgely, etc...

The German Element in Virginia: Herrmann Schuricht's History

The German Immigrant in America

The Pennsylvania Germans: James Owen Knauss, Jr.'s Social History

The Pennsylvania Germans: Jesse Leonard Rosenberger's Sketch of Their History and Life

Made in the USA